Trusting God with St. Therese

Connie Rossini

FOUR WATERS PRESS
NEW ULM, MINNESOTA

© 2014 Four Waters Press
217 South Jefferson Street
New Ulm, Minnesota 56073

Ordering Information:
Special discounts are available on quantity purchases by parishes, book clubs, associations, and others. For details, contact the publisher at the address above.

Printed in the United States of America

First Printing, 2014

ISBN-13: 978-0692248522

To Mom and Dad,
in thanksgiving for your love and example
that set me firmly on the narrow way.

About the Author

Connie Rossini lives with her husband Dan in New Ulm, Minnesota, where she homeschools their four sons. Her spirituality column is published in *The Prairie Catholic* of the Diocese of New Ulm and *The Catholic Times* of La Crosse, Wisconsin. She is the author of the free e-book *Five Lessons from the Carmelite Saints That Will Change Your Life.* Connie spent seventeen years as a member of the Secular Order of Discalced Carmelites. She blogs on Carmelite spirituality and raising prayerful kids at contemplativehomeschool.com. She is a columnist at SpiritualDirection.com, and also administers Catholic Spirituality Blogs Network.

Contents

Abbreviations

CCC *Catechism of the Catholic Church*. Libreria Editrice Vaticana—United States Conference of Catholic Bishops, 1994.

EW *St. Thérèse of Lisieux: Essential Writings*. Mary Frohlich. Maryknoll, NY: Orbis Books, Institute for Carmelite Studies, 2003.

HF *The Hidden Face: A Study of St. Thérèse of Lisieux*. Ida Friederike Gorres. Translated by Richard and Clara Wintson. San Francisco: Ignatius Press, 2003.

LC *St. Thérèse: Her Last Conversations*. Translated by John Clarke, OCD. Washington, DC: ICS Publications, Institute for Carmelite Studies, 1977.

LT *The Letters of St. Thérèse of Lisieux and Those Who Knew Her: General Correspondence*. Translated by John Clarke, OCD. 2 vols. Washington, DC: ICS Publications, Institute for Carmelite Studies, 2002.

NPPA Notes prepared for the Apostolic Process. Translated by Association des Amis de Thérèse de Lisieux et de son Carmel.

NPPO Notes prepared for the Ordinary Process. Translated by Association des Amis de Thérèse de Lisieux et de son Carmel.

PT *The Passion of Thérèse of Lisieux*. Guy Gaucher. Translated by Sr. Anne Marie Brennan, OCD. Homebush, NSW, Australia: St. Paul Publications, 1989.

SL *Story of a Life: St. Thérèse of Lisieux*. Guy Gaucher. Translated by Sr. Anne Marie Brennan, OCD. San Francisco: Harper & Row, 1987.

SP *Spiritual Passages: the Psychology of Spiritual Development*. Benedict J. Groeschel. New York: The Crossroad Publishing Co., 1983.

SS *Story of a Soul: the Autobiography of St. Thérèse of Lisieux*. Translated by John Clarke, OCD. Washington, DC: ICS Publications, Institute for Carmelite Studies, 1996.

SS2 *Story of a Soul: the Autobiography of St. Thérèse of Lisieux*. Edited by Rev. T. N. Taylor. London: Burns, Oates & Washbourne, 1912; 8th ed., 1922. http://www.ccel.org/ccel/therese/autobio.

STL *Saint Thérèse of Lisieux: Her Family, Her God, Her Message*. Fr. Bernard Bro. Translated by Anne Englund Nash. San Francisco: Ignatius Press, 2003.

TF *The Father of the Little Flower*. Sr. Genevieve of the Holy Face. Charlotte: St. Benedict Press, LLC, 2009, excerpted by the publisher at http://www.tanbooks.com/doct/father_little_flower.htm.

TL *Therese and Lisieux*. Pierre Descouvement. Photographed by Helmuth Nils Loose. Translated by Salvatore Sciurba and Louise Pambrun. Grand Rapids: Wm. B. Eerdman's, 1996.

TT *Thoughts of Saint Therese*. Translated by an Irish Carmelite. Rockford, IL: Tan Books and Publishers, Inc., (1915) 1988.

ZM *A Short Life of Blessed Zelie Martin, Mother of St. Thérèse*. J. Linus Ryan, O Carm, web.archive.org/web/20120315073852/http://www.sttherese.com/Parents.html

Preface

I must see her real life, not her imagined life.

St. Therese of Lisieux, speaking about St. Joan of Arc (PT)

When dramatizing the story of St. Therese, I sometimes slightly paraphrased her or others' words as written by the witnesses to her life. At other times, I created dialog based on the available text. In a few places, I added possible conversation that might have occurred before Therese spoke the words that were written down. Whenever I quoted directly from another source in my dialog, I cited the source. When I paraphrased dialog, I wrote, "(See . . .)," citing the source afterwards. All dialog without citation is my creation.

Citations from complete letters in the two-volume *Letters of St. Thérèse* are noted by letter number, except for the excerpts at the back of Volume II, which I note by page number. These excerpts were not numbered in the original.

For ease of reading, I excluded accent marks in French names, except those which aid my English-speaking readers in pronunciation, or when I cite a title which includes them.

All punctuation, capitalization, and emphasis are from the original texts, unless otherwise noted.

Introduction

Fear not, for I am with you, be not dismayed, for I am your God; I will strengthen you, I will help you, I will uphold you with my victorious right hand.

Is 41:10

Recently I began posing this question to new subscribers to my blog: "What's the main thing in your life that is holding you back from God?" Here are some of the answers I have received:

"Anger and time management."

"Lack of focus in my spiritual life."

"Inconsistency."

"Fear and a lack of trust."

"I feel guilty and sad about leaving Lay Carmelites."

"I don't trust God completely."

"I get bored, tired, distracted, and overwhelmed by my daily life."

One new reader wrote, "I made a huge spiritual jump about five to seven years ago, but now I feel stagnant. I want to take another leap."

And then another reader answered, "Nothing."

This book is for people who want to be holy, but find their spiritual life stagnating. My hope is to help you move from stagnation to the place where "nothing" is holding you back from God. Not your fears or your guilt or your weakness or your anger.

Trusting God with St. Therese is different from the spiritual books you have read before. It is practical and specific. It is geared toward people who are already doing the basics of following God, but who want something more. People who want to be saints. And it is written with the average reader in mind, not scholars or theologians.

Until a short time ago, I too was overwhelmed by the number of things I had to think about in my vocation and in my spiritual life. I was angry, fearful, disappointed, and distraught. I expected my way to be smoother. I expected to reach higher stages of spirituality more quickly. I did not know how to get out of my rut.

Then I began to focus intently on trusting God. What did St. Therese teach about trust? More than that, how did she live it out? How could I take her example, the example of a nineteenth century Carmelite nun, and apply it to my life as a twenty-first century wife and mother?

I had started blogging just a couple of months before this. I blogged about my reflections on trust, my efforts—and sometimes my failures—to follow the little way of spiritual childhood. And my life began to change.

Now I invite you more deeply into my struggles. I want to share with you my lifetime struggle to trust God, starting with my earliest days. I will show you how, reflecting on each stage of St. Therese's life, I found an echo in mine.

Our cultures, our families, our vocations were different. But our human nature and our purpose in life were the same. I found surprising help through such things as Therese's petitioning the pope to enter the cloister early. I realized her role as assistant novice mistress in Carmel was similar to my role as mother and teacher of my sons. We both had to deal with childhood tragedies, waiting for God's plan to be fulfilled, fears for our loved ones, and questions about death and eternity.

As a writer and a teacher, I know the power of stories. Stories inspire us. They move our hearts. Each chapter begins with a true story from the life of St. Therese, told in narrative form, sticking as closely to known facts as possible. The chapters progress more or less sequentially from her birth to her death. Each chapter includes a corresponding story from my life as well. I have changed some people's names in my memoirs, but the stories are true.

Woven among the stories are insights from the *Catechism of the Catholic Church,* Sacred Scripture, other spiritual writings, and psychology. These insights help you dig deeper, to grasp the meaning of St. Therese's example.

Finally, questions for reflection and practical suggestions move you to apply the lessons to your life. They can form the groundwork of your road to trusting God.

At the end of the book you'll find A Brief Timeline of the Life of St. Therese, as well as Who's Who in the Life of St. Therese. These additions should help you keep the characters and events in her life straight so they don't hinder your understanding of her message.

As you read this book, remember that you are trusting God *with* St. Therese—not just according to her teaching. In heaven she cheers you on. She prays for you. As she promised, she showers roses down upon you. She wants you to succeed. And so does God.

> If God is for us, who is against us? He who did not spare his own Son but gave him up for us all, will he not also give us all things with him? . . . We are more than conquerors. . . . For I am sure that neither death, nor life, nor angels, nor principalities, nor things present, nor things to come, nor powers, nor height, nor depth, nor anything else in all creation, will be able to separate us from the love of God in Christ Jesus our Lord. (Rom 8:31–32, 37, 38–39)

You can conquer your fear, anger, and anxiety with the help of God's grace. You can learn to trust God perfectly. Someday, when someone asks you what is holding you back from following God whole heartedly, you too can answer, "Nothing."

Chapter One
The Importance of Trusting God

Trust in the Lord with all your heart, and do not rely on your own insight.
In all your ways acknowledge him, and he will make straight your path.
Prov 3:5–6

In the Carmelite monastery in Lisieux, France, a young nun lay dying. She had coughed up blood twice that day. The brown habit hung limply on her shrinking frame. Even her hands were skeleton-like. Her face was flushed with fever. Sharp pains pierced her right lung. At times she struggled to breathe. She was too weak to raise her hand to her mouth.

Dr. Alexandre-Damase de Corniere refused to allow the nuns to bring her downstairs to the infirmary for fear the movement would kill her. He ordered her to stay perfectly still and prescribed sucking on ice cubes to stop the coughing up of blood. He also ordered mustard poultices.

Sr. Therese of the Child Jesus and the Holy Face had been seriously ill since the early morning hours of Good Friday, nearly fifteen months before. Returning to her cell after Compline, the Church's Night Prayer, she had coughed up blood for the first time. She was certain then that she was to die soon. However, she hid her illness as long as she could. She dragged herself to choir, worked in the laundry, and sewed vestments. No one knew the effort this cost her. Only the previous spring was she relieved of all duties besides finishing the manuscript she was writing about her life.

Then in June came a night so bad that the doctor predicted she would not survive. But Therese rallied. Her condition stabilized until this crisis of July 6, 1897.

On July 8, Dr. de Corniere examined her again. Seeing her continued weakness, he shook his head. "In this condition, only two percent recover," he told Mother Marie de Gonzague, the prioress. He said that Therese had congestion in an injured lung, although the ultimate diagnosis was tuberculosis.

Therese heard his words and smiled. Perhaps at last she could receive Extreme Unction! She had been asking for it for weeks. In those days the Anointing of the Sick (as we now call it) was only given when death was thought to be imminent.

Therese turned to Mother Agnes of Jesus, her older sister, the former Pauline Martin. Mother Agnes was often with her these days. She had even received permission to miss praying Matins (known as Morning Prayer in English, although the nuns prayed it at 9 P.M.) with the rest of the community, to spend more time with Therese.

"I want to be anointed very much," Therese said to her. "Let them laugh at me afterwards if they want to" (LC 81). She suspected that if she rallied again some of the sisters would think she had never really been in danger. Even now, after she had been suffering for months, many in the convent did not believe she was seriously ill. She never complained and remained in good spirits, telling jokes to keep her companions from being sad.

Mother Agnes helped Therese examine her conscience. Then Therese confessed her sins to Abbé Youf, the convent's confessor.

After receiving absolution, Therese glanced around her cell for the last time. How many graces God had given her there! But she was nonetheless happy to leave it, since she would be going soon to meet him face to face.

The sisters carried her down to the infirmary on her mattress, even though the doctor had still not given them permission to move her. With her were Mother Agnes, Sr. Marie of the Sacred Heart (their eldest sister Marie), and Sr. Marie of the Eucharist (their cousin Marie Guerin). Celine, the fourth Martin sister to enter Carmel, was now Sr. Genevieve. She was assistant to the infirmarian, who let her tend Therese. Genevieve slept in a cell attached to the infirmary, on call to help patients day and night. Of the Martin sisters then, only Leonie—who had made three unsuccessful attempts to join other orders and was now living with their uncle and aunt—was unable to be with Therese in her last days.

The nuns moved the statue of the Virgin of the Smile to the infirmary ahead of them. Our Lady used this statue to cure Therese from a serious illness when she was ten. Therese customarily kept the statue in an anteroom to her cell, where she met with the novices in her charge. As the nuns placed the mattress with Therese on it gently on the bed frame, she looked towards the statue with an expression her family members could not interpret.

"What do you see?" asked Marie of the Sacred Heart. Therese had confided her miraculous cure as a child to Marie alone. Marie hoped for another miraculous intervention now. After all, the convent was in the middle of praying a novena to Our Lady of Victories for a cure.

Therese replied, "She looks more beautiful to me than ever. But I am only speaking about the statue, not like that other day, when it was the Virgin herself." (See the Authentic Digital Classics edition of *The Story of a Soul: A New Translation.*) God did not grant Therese miracles, visions, or consolations now. He left her to the same physical and ordinary comforts as the rest of her Carmelite family.

A painting of the Holy Face of Jesus hung on the wall outside the door, the namesake of both the infirmary and Therese. Pictures of her favorite intercessors were pinned to the brown bed curtains. There was Theophane Villard (a recent martyr whom she admired), Joan of Arc, the four Martin children who had died in childhood, and of course the Blessed Virgin Mary. Therese would feel at home here for the short time she hoped to stay.

Mother Agnes remained by her side, catching up every word Therese spoke as though it were a holy relic, and recording it on any piece of paper she could find. A year earlier, when Mother Agnes was prioress, she had directed Therese to write about her childhood memories. In obedience, Therese wrote the first part of her autobiography. We know it today as Manuscript A of *Story of a Soul.* Mother Agnes did not read it immediately. When she finally did, she realized that her sister was a saint. Instead of just family stories, the manuscript was filled with spiritual wisdom. Now Mother Agnes spent her time asking Therese about her spirituality, her experiences, and her spiritual darkness. She wanted to learn everything she could about Therese's little way of spiritual childhood before it was too late.

Although suffering greatly, Therese brimmed with joy that day. She rattled on about heaven at amazing length for one who was supposed to be dying. "Oh, certainly, I shall cry when I see God!" she said to Mother Agnes, before correcting herself. "No, we can't cry in heaven. Yes, we can, since it is said: 'And God will wipe away every tear from their eyes'" (LC 81). The tears of her short life had been many.

"I wish I could be as certain of going straight to heaven as you are," remarked Marie of the Eucharist. "But I've never been good like you. I know I'll have to spend time in Purgatory."

If Therese could have sat up and taken her cousin by the arms, she would have done so. They had been close friends since childhood. Marie Guerin had always followed Therese's lead. Therese had directed her in the novitiate as well. But she contented herself with replying, "Oh, how you grieve me! You do a great injury to God in believing you're going to go to Purgatory. When we love, we can't go there" (LC 273).

The following day, July 9, Dr. de Corniere visited twice. He found that her symptoms had declined slightly.

When Canon Charles Maupas, the nuns' superior, observed how cheerful and strong Therese appeared, he chose not to give her the Anointing of the Sick. He doubted she was on the verge of death. And he was proved right. For although Therese soon grew worse again and could keep nothing down—not even the condensed milk that served as her medicine—she had to wait a while longer to see God.

Therese was disappointed, but remained peaceful and resigned. God had made her wait for him before. She would accept his will without a murmur. "The 'Thief' is still absent!" she said to Marie of the Sacred Heart, referring to Jesus' coming as a Thief in the night. This had become a favorite way of talking about death with her sisters. "Well, as God wills it" (LC 237).

She had told Mother Agnes on July 7, "This saying of Job: 'Although he should kill me, I will trust in him,' has fascinated me from my childhood. But it took me a long time before I was established in this degree of abandonment. Now I am there; God has placed me there. He took me into His arms and placed me there" (LC 77). Death and life were all the same to her. She trusted completely in God's providence.

Can we attain the same level of trust?

Before starting out on the road to trusting God, we ask the obvious question: Is perfect trust attainable for us? Do we need to practice it? Can we? In this chapter, we'll see the importance of trust for our spiritual lives. I'll show how my lack of trust threatened my relationship with Christ. Fr. Benedict Groeschel will teach us where trust fits into the usual pattern of spiritual growth. Finally, we'll consider several signs of distrust.

Therese's trust in God is almost legendary—so much so that we might consider such trust beyond our reach. In her family and later in the Carmelite cloister, she was bathed in a culture focused on Christ. When she struggled at school, she came home to learn among those who understood her. When she wanted to give herself fully to God, she became a nun. When she began to speak about her little way of spiritual childhood, others encouraged her.

We daily encounter challenges to trust that she never faced. The world around us—sometimes even including our dearest family members—meets our desire for God with indifference or hostility. In the Church, others think us presumptuous for even striving to follow God more faithfully. And an insistent voice inside us urges us at every step to abandon our course.

Why focus on trust? we ask ourselves. There are so many pressing problems for Catholics in today's world: battling the Culture of Death, bringing strays back to the faith, revamping catechesis, caring for the poor. Why not focus instead on one of these?

When we ponder this question more deeply, the mistaken notion behind it reveals itself. We do not practice one virtue or join an apostolate in isolation from the rest of our Christian life. Focusing on trust does not take us away from these other important things. It helps us advance in them. Fighting the Culture of Death, for example, can be discouraging, heartbreaking, and personally risky. Trust gives us the strength to persevere. Likewise, we must trust God with the hearts of the lost, for ultimately only he can convert them. We must trust him to work through his Church, even when the humans who make up that Church fall short. And unless we can accept God's providence, the trials of the poor will crush our spirits.

Why should we focus on trust? In a letter to Marie of the Sacred Heart, Therese put it concisely: "It is trust, and nothing but trust that must bring us to Love" (PT 61). "Love," of course, is God himself. In other words, we cannot grow close to him until we trust him.

But wait, we say, *wasn't Therese exaggerating?* Did she really mean *"nothing* but trust" would lead us to God?

Trust was no minor theme in Therese's life. From the beginning, the Holy Spirit seems to have chosen her to be an apostle of trust, to teach us what it really means to trust God. Therese followed the road of love to its very end. This road of love was her little way. Trust guided her, preventing her from stalling or veering off course.

"What offends Jesus," she wrote in her first preserved letter to Marie Guerin, "what wounds Him to the Heart, is want of confidence" (TT 82). Marie at that time was suffering from scruples that tempted her to avoid receiving Communion. Therese was certain that her cousin's lack of trust in God's mercy would offend him more than any little sin she might have committed when she was striving to follow him. Therese had faced the same temptation and God had shown her the solution. The proper response to our weaknesses is trust.

Now, does that mean that only trust is necessary for the spiritual life, that the other virtues will get us nowhere? Not exactly. Other virtues will get us somewhere, but if trust does not accompany them, our spiritual growth will come to an end. We must let go of control over our spiritual lives in order to be saints. Let's face it, such control is an illusion anyway. But God will not force us to give it up. He requires us to surrender it willingly. We must give God the freedom to work his will in his own way and time, and that means trusting him.

Getting stuck in the spiritual life

Like us, Therese was born imperfect, wounded by Original Sin. At each stage of her life, each challenge, she had to choose to trust, just as we do. I have just begun to realize how much her life had in common with all of ours. I can grow in trust by meditating on my past and present, asking how my challenges parallel hers.

"Inspired by the Holy Spirit, and in response to God's call, I, Mary Francis of the Divine Mercy, sincerely promise to the Superiors of the Order of Teresian Carmel, and to you, my brothers and sisters, to tend toward evangelical perfection in the spirit of the evangelical counsels of chastity, poverty, and obedience, and of the Beatitudes, according to the Rule of the Secular Order of Discalced Carmelites, for three years. I confidently entrust this, my promise, to the Blessed Virgin Mary, Mother and Queen of Carmel."

Kneeling in the sanctuary of St. Raphael's Church in Crystal, Minnesota, I recited these words. Along with several women of various ages and one older man, I was making my temporary promise as a Secular Carmelite.

At that time, the order encouraged members to choose the names of two saints and a devotion, which we could use in place of our own names in official Carmelite arenas. I had chosen to be named for the Blessed Virgin Mary and St. Francis de Sales. In our daily lives we would still go by our given names.

The Discalced Carmelites are the branch of the Carmelite family established by St. Teresa of Avila and St. John of the Cross. Therese was a Discalced Carmelite nun. The Secular Order (OCDS) provides a way for lay people and parish priests to be closely associated with the nuns and friars of Carmel.

For a long time I had felt the Holy Spirit prompting me to join a Christian community of some kind. I was raised in a Catholic charismatic household, as part of a closely-knit community that was like extended family. But that no longer seemed the right fit for me. I was drawn towards more traditional expressions of Catholicism. When I read a little booklet called *How to Avoid Purgatory* by Fr. Paul O'Sullivan, I learned of the graces offered to secular members of various orders. I was determined to avoid Purgatory at all costs, so I began practicing a few of Fr. O'Sullivan's suggestions. Among other things, I decided I should research secular orders. But months passed and I did not pursue this.

Then at a party a friend held for Catholic singles, I met a young woman who was an OCDS novice. Coincidentally, her community was meeting the next day. She invited me to join her. How could I say *no?* God was so obviously doing for me the work I had failed to do.

I attended the three-hour meeting and immediately felt Carmel was where I belonged.

Like the friars and nuns, Secular Carmelites have at least six years of formation before making a lifelong promise. In rare instances, some members also take a vow of poverty and obedience after their final promise. As I moved through formation, I studied prayer and the practice of virtue. I reread the writings of some of my favorite saints, this time with people who could explain to me what I had missed when I read them on my own.

I recommitted to praying mental prayer daily. I learned to live a simpler life. I began practicing detachment. Soon God's work in my prayer time became obvious. I felt closer to him than ever. I was happy and at peace.

As I made my promise, I was leaving the novitiate behind. I rose from my knees and adjusted the large brown scapular that we wore for ceremonial occasions. One side or the other was constantly slipping off a shoulder. Our daily habit was the much smaller, simple brown scapular—two small cloth rectangles connected with string, worn under the clothes. I had worn one for years, double knotted to shorten its length. Doing that would have been more difficult with the white ribbons that held the large scapular together. Besides, it would have looked ridiculous knotted over my dress clothes.

Both scapulars were crafted by the Carmelite nuns in Lake Elmo. They were made to fit the average adult. When you are less than five feet tall, average sizes drown you.

Being short sometimes annoyed me. It meant being unable to drive some compact cars, using stepstools in the kitchen, buying petite clothes (and still finding them too big), being treated like a child—and having scapulars slip off my shoulders.

When all the candidates had finished reciting the promise, the congregation applauded. Then we returned to our pews. My parents, along with my older sister Julie who happened to be in town that week, and my roommate Sarah, had all come to celebrate with me. I beamed at them as I slipped back to my place.

Someone in our community had said that on the day you make your promise, you can ask God for anything and he will grant it to you. He blesses those who give their lives to him in this way. So, besides asking for the return of loved ones to the Church, I made two more requests of God. I asked that within a year I might meet my future husband. I was thirty-one years old and growing anxious about my primary vocation. I also asked that I might become holy.

God answered the first of these. Almost a year to the day later, I met Dan Rossini.

But as for the second petition, instead of moving forward in the spiritual life, I got stuck. The peace disappeared. My commitment to praying every day never wavered, but my prayer itself stagnated. While still trying to be virtuous, I was no longer measurably growing, and I may even have gone backwards in some areas. This was no passing phase. I struggled this way for years.

As time passed, Dan and I married and had four sons. I made my definitive (lifelong) promise as a Secular Carmelite. But I was still in a spiritual slump. I grew more and more distraught about my spiritual life.

Then Dan bought me *The Way of Trust and Love* by Fr. Jacques Philippe as a birthday present. The book, which presents the little way Therese devised, from the perspective of trust and love, didn't immediately draw me in. But somewhere near the middle of the book, the audacity of Therese's trust in God and its significance for my life became clear.

My eyes were opened. The root of my problem was simple, though I had not seen it. I did not want to be little. I did not acknowledge that I *was* little. I did not realize that I *needed to be* little. Quite ironic, for a Carmelite.

Months later, I discovered that my experience of hitting a spiritual rut and needing a new direction was a common one. Spiritual directors have long noted this pattern. Some have even coined terms to describe it.

The three conversions of the purgative way

Catholic theologians divide the spiritual life into three major stages. We can get stuck any place along the journey to God, but especially in the transitions between these stages. Each new stage calls for a change in perspective, one that's not always easy to grasp.

The first stage, known as the purgative way, is a time of purification from sin and attachments. The second stage is the illuminative way. In this stage God enlightens the mind to know his will more clearly and gives the gift of supernatural contemplation. The final stage is the unitive way, in which a person is almost constantly aware of God's presence. At last he has the power to closely conform himself to God's will.

St. Teresa of Avila, a doctor of the Church like Therese herself, wrote a master work about growth in prayer called *Interior Castle*. She envisioned the soul as a castle having seven rooms or mansions. Each mansion represented a different stage of the spiritual life. The first three mansions are generally considered to belong to the purgative way.

Souls do not necessarily progress sequentially through the seven mansions, but wander more freely among them. They can even be in two different mansions at the same time in two different areas of their life. Likewise, purgation continues throughout our lives, even after we have long been contemplatives. We will not be completely free from sin and attachments until the end of life or the end of our stay in Purgatory.

In his book *Spiritual Passages: the Psychology of Spiritual Development,* Fr. Benedict Groeschel further breaks down the purgative way. He identifies three conversions that must take place in order for the soul to be completely purified. Each of the three conversions roughly corresponds to one of St. Teresa's first three mansions.

The first conversion is from mortal sin or Original Sin to a state of grace. At this stage we learn the commandments and try to follow them. Fr. Groeschel notes that children, consciously or not, bargain with God. They think that if they are good, God will "be good" back to them. But they eventually learn that God does not give them everything they want. He does not always answer their prayers as they would like or expect.

At this point, a person could choose to abandon the faith, because he expected something different. Many people who are hostile to Christianity have left the faith at this stage. They don't really understand what the Christian life is about. They might think God is unfair. They might picture God as a sort of fairy-godfather whom only fools would believe in. They are rejecting their childhood notion of God, never realizing that their Christian friends and family have moved beyond that notion.

This realization that God does not always intervene in the world as we ask him to also brings the opportunity for the second conversion. Those who continue on enter the stage Fr. Groeschel calls mature faith. They become passionate about following God. People who have recently experienced this conversion often think they have "arrived" spiritually.

They think they are nearly saints. On the contrary, they are just beginning.

The Christian in this stage has a much deeper understanding of God and his ways than he did before. He learns that God doesn't fit into neat human categories. He realizes there are some questions he cannot answer, some ways of God he cannot understand. Yet he believes in God more strongly than ever. His prayer moves from childish requests and vocal prayers to meditation on Sacred Scripture. Then gradually he finds himself spending less time speaking or thinking in prayer and more time sitting quietly in God's presence.

Then another crisis occurs. Perhaps a loved one dies, or a person experiences another tragedy. Or he encounters apparently insurmountable problems in his struggle against sin. He sees evil at work in his life or in the world, and he must come to terms with it. Once again, he can leave, he can stagnate, or he can grow.

Finally, there is a conversion to perfect trust in God. The person lets go of his anxiety and fear. He places absolute trust in God, even when it seems that everything is going wrong. He realizes that God is in charge of the world and of his spiritual growth. He learns to be at peace among all the storms of life. He abandons himself to divine providence as Jesus did in the garden of Gethsemane.

Signs of a lack of trust

Distrust can manifest itself in a myriad of ways: anger, anxiety, being lukewarm, boredom, cheating, complaining, discouragement, dissatisfaction, envy, excessive reserve, fantasizing, fear, gluttony, hoarding, hopelessness, jealousy, judging, lack of close relationships, low self-esteem, lying, presumption, pride, stealing, stinginess, and unwillingness to make sacrifices.

Distrust keeps us focused on ourselves, rather than on God and others. It prevents us from fully obeying the two greatest commandments: loving God with our whole being and loving our neighbor as ourselves. Self-absorption makes holiness impossible.

In other words, trust is necessary for us to enter into heaven. If we do not learn to trust God fully here on earth, he will have to cleanse us of our distrust in Purgatory. We will not receive what we hope for until that hope has been perfected.

Questions for Reflection

1. In what state is my spiritual life? Am I moving forward, spinning my wheels, or falling backward?

2. Am I open to looking at the spiritual life from a new perspective? What might be giving me pause at this moment?

3. Do I believe that trust is necessary for continued growth toward God? What experiences in my life appear to confirm or deny this?

4. Where am I in terms of the three conversions of the purgative way?

5. How could increasing my trust in God improve my spiritual life?

Practical Suggestions

* Examine your conscience as you would in preparation for Reconciliation. Make a list of the sins and failings that seem to plague you regularly. How many of them may be related to trust? Keep this list handy as you read the rest of this book.

* Write, "It is trust and nothing but trust that must bring us to Love" on a note card. Place it where you will see it daily.

Chapter Two
A Second Chance at Trusting

But all who have received him, to them—that is, to those who trust in his name—he has given the privilege of becoming children of God.

Jn 1:4

Marie-Azelie Guerin Martin, while still a young woman, had injured her breast in a fall. The pain endured through the years. She breastfed her first four daughters without incident, but when she tried to nurse her other children, difficulties plagued her. Two infant sons succumbed to inflammation of the small intestine and died, one after the other. Daughter Celine was sent out to three different wet nurses before a suitable one was found. At one point, she nearly starved to death. The wet nurse in charge of the eighth child, Marie-Melanie-Therese, turned out to be an alcoholic who neglected her. The Martins learned about it too late to save the child. She died of malnutrition at two months old.

In addition, a little daughter named Helene who was cherished by the whole family died of a sudden illness at age five.

Zelie, as Marie-Azelie was known, longed to have another daughter after her eighth baby's death. She discovered she was expecting once more when she was forty years old. She knew this was likely to be her last child. She feared hiring a wet nurse again (LT 1198–99).

Baby Marie-Françoise-Therese started out strong. Some said she was a full eight pounds at birth, though Zelie estimated the newborn's weight was closer to six (SL 7). Therese almost immediately caused her parents anxiety. When she was two weeks old, Zelie gave in to fear and fed her from a bottle. Then Therese temporarily refused to nurse. When she started taking long naps, Zelie grew frightened. Her boys had slept similarly long as their health deteriorated. These anxieties were passing, however. They may never have had any substance to them.

Then in March 1873, only two months after her birth, Therese's health noticeably declined. She was soon diagnosed with the same illness that had caused her brothers' deaths. Although pale, she was not thin, and retained her smile and laughter, which she had displayed uncommonly early.

Conventional wisdom said Therese should be given over to a wet nurse. Instead, Zelie tried some home remedies to bring her back to health. But what she needed was breast milk, and she was not getting enough from her mother. As Therese continued to get worse, Zelie called in Dr. Pierre Hippolyte Belloc on the evening of March 10.

Dr. Belloc examined Therese and was immediately concerned. "This baby needs more nutrition," he said. "Give her one spoonful of rice water and one of lime water in two spoonfuls of milk, twice a day. But you must also find a wet nurse for her." (See LT 1203.)

Who was there in Alençon Zelie could trust with Therese? After the doctor left, Zelie paced the floor, mentally discarding the options one by one. She and her husband Louis had been through this before Therese's birth. They could think of no one suitable. Every available wet nurse was either of questionable character or otherwise unreliable.

Then she considered Rose Taillé, who had nursed two of her other children. Rose and her family lived on a farm outside the village of Semallé, about five miles from Alençon. Zelie knew Rose was nursing her own child, so wet nursing would be possible. However, that child was a year older than Therese, due to be weaned soon, and Zelie thought

Rose's milk might be "too old" for a tiny infant. She decided she must consult the doctor again.

At 11 P.M. she went to see Dr. Belloc to ask him about it, leaving Therese with a servant. (The oldest Martin daughters were away at boarding school at the time.) The doctor listened to Zelie's story with pursed lips. "You must take her to Semallé immediately," he said when she had finished. "It is the only option you have now for saving your child" (ibid.).

Still, Zelie hesitated. Louis was out of town, and there was no other family member she could ask for help. She could not travel to Semallé by herself in the middle of the night. And even if she did, how could she wake the Taillé household? She would wait until morning. Surely there would still be enough time!

She attempted to nurse Therese herself when she returned home, but the child would take nothing.

Zelie lay Therese on the red velvet bedspread in the parents' room and watched her. What a lovely child God had given them! Her golden hair encircled her head like a halo. But she had at last grown thin.

Zelie sat down beside her on the edge of the bed. Her hand strayed to the lace collar that adorned her own dress, absently rubbing it between her thumb and forefinger. It was of own her making, her own, intricate, beautiful design. In her lace shop, Zelie was in control, assigning pieces to other townswomen to create. She would later lace them together so skillfully that no one could tell they were not one whole piece (TL 15). She was a successful business woman, an admired artisan.

And yet she was helpless.

Throughout the night she put Therese to her breast several times, but the baby still refused to eat. There was nothing Zelie could do, except wait until morning.

As soon as it was light, she once again left the children with a servant, and set out on foot alone, heading for the home of Rose Taillé. It was cold and dark, and the road was lonely. Nothing could deter her now—not even a pair of men she encountered as she walked alone, although normally she would have been frightened. Every minute mattered.

The Taillé family lived in a small brick farmhouse with a thatched roof. They had apple trees, pastures, and land for crops.

Zelie banged on the wooden front door. A surprised Rose opened it. She had the broad face and dark skin of a peasant woman. Her hair was tied up in a white kerchief.

"Please, come back to Alençon with me and nurse my baby," Zelie pleaded. "She's so frail and she won't eat anything. The doctor says I must get a wet nurse at once."

Rose was not willing to leave her family. "I'm still nursing my own baby," she said. "And who will take care of our other three? I'm sorry. You'll have to find someone else."

Zelie would not give up. She knew Rose was Therese's only hope. "There is no one else. Please, Rose. Hear me as a mother. This is my child, the last one I'm likely to have. You can arrange it any way you want. Bring Therese back here, if you must. But don't refuse to help me. She'll starve to death without your assistance."

Rose was moved, in spite of herself. At last, after consulting with her husband, she agreed to spend a week with the Martins, and then bring Therese back to live on the farm.

The two women walked back to Alençon together. The road seemed even longer than before. Zelie was completely exhausted, but dared not delay any longer. When they arrived at the Martin home, it was already 10:30 A.M. Therese still had not had anything to eat or drink. Rose took one look at her thin, pale body and shook her head, saying, "It is too late. I have made a useless trip" (LT 1204).

But Zelie thrust the baby into Rose's arms, urging her to try feeding Therese, despite her lack of hope. Then she ran upstairs to her room and threw herself on her knees before a statue of St. Joseph. She begged the saint who had protected the infant Christ from harm to spare her daughter. Must she bear the death of a fifth child? How could Louis, who had been heartbroken by the loss of Helene, endure coming home to find little Therese gone as well? Zelie was a firm and strong woman, not easily moved by emotion. But now tears streamed down her face as she tried to resign herself to God's will. She must be ready to accept anything. "Therese is yours, God," she whispered. "Do with her as you will." Then she rose, wiped her tears and smoothed her skirt, and returned downstairs.

Her heart was pounding in her chest as she re-entered the room where she had left Rose and Therese. Would she find Therese already dead? To her surprise, the baby was nursing hungrily.

Therese continued eating for hours. At last she latched off and spit up twice. Then her head fell back against Rose, her eyes closed. She was perfectly still. She did not even appear to be breathing. For fifteen minutes Zelie and Rose fixed their eyes on her, barely breathing themselves as they watched for signs of life. Behind Zelie the servant wept.

Silently and slowly, Zelie prayed a Hail Mary, then another. Suddenly Therese's eyes fluttered open and she smiled.

"Oh, thank God!" Zelie exclaimed. "She's alive!"

Rose took Therese home to Semallé once she had stabilized, as they had agreed. Therese stayed there for thirteen months, growing in strength and learning to love the countryside. A further tragedy had been prevented.

Memories of love

For some of us, distrust has been a constant companion, seemingly from the first moment of our lives. Where did this distrust originate? This chapter explores the psychological and spiritual roots of our distrust. We'll look briefly at Erik Erikson's theory of psycho-social development, as well as the role trust played in Adam's sin. I'll share an early memory of an event that fostered my distrust. We'll see that we do not have to remain prisoners of our past. We'll learn to move beyond blaming others for our lack of trust to changing our hearts. God offers us a second chance at trusting.

Therese had an unusually positive family experience. She was blessed with parents who not only loved her, but who were striving for sanctity. In fact, Pope Benedict XVI beatified Louis and Zelie Martin in 2008. Their canonizations will require that the Church accept one more miracle for each of them. They were loving parents, active in their children's lives. Therese wrote, "God gave me a father and a mother more worthy of Heaven than of earth; they asked the Lord to give them many children and to take them for Himself. This desire was answered: four little angels flew away to Heaven, and five children left in the arena took Jesus for Bridegroom" (LT 261).

The Martins dealt in a healthy manner with the tragedies of losing their four children. Through their suffering, they learned to trust God's plan, even when it was beyond their understanding, even when it caused them pain. Before Therese could talk, she was surrounded by the language of trust.

She also had the prime spot in the family for learning love and trust. She was the youngest of five sisters. Gifted with an incredible recall, she later wrote, "My first memories are of smiles and loving caresses" (SS 22).

Therese soaked up the love that she received. She gave it back abundantly to others and to God.

She does not mention the health problems she experienced in infancy in her autobiography *Story of a Soul.* However, some authors speculate that the double removal from her mother to her wet nurse and back again left a scar on her heart (see EW 18–19).

Zelie's letters detail Therese's difficulties. Rose Taillé sold butter and other goods in the market weekly. Rose either dropped Therese off at the Martin home, or Zelie and some of the other children visited Therese at the farm. Each time, Therese cried unceasingly, until her mother brought her to the market to see Rose. Then she stopped at once. She later went through months of readjustment when she returned home for good.

This disruption in her attachment to her mother could not have been good for Therese, even if the use of wet nurses was common among the bourgeois of the time, especially where the mother or child had health problems. We could criticize Zelie's decisions regarding Therese and her other children. A twenty-first century doctor would never give the advice Dr. Belloc did. But the Martins lived in an age before infant formula. The causes of many ailments of infancy were not well understood. We cannot judge her by today's parenting standards.

Even the godliest parents cannot fully protect their children from threats to trust.

Trust versus mistrust

The first two years of a child's life form a crucial period for learning to trust. Psychologist Erik Erikson identified several stages of psychosocial development that are now standardly used by child development experts. In each stage, an individual faces a "critical conflict" (SP 40). He either embraces a positive lesson that becomes part of his maturing self-identity, or he embraces its opposite. The first stage lasts roughly from birth to eighteen months. Trust and mistrust form the conflict. If a child learns to trust, he will be ready to move on to the next stage. If he does not learn to trust, he could have problems with fear and mistrust for the rest of his life, and future development may be stunted.

Some people have such difficult childhoods that it is no surprise they do not learn to trust others. Spending their first few years without steady parents or loving caregivers, they might never be able to connect with others in a healthy manner. They may have enduring difficulty trusting that God or other human beings will be there for them. They could develop a serious psychological condition called Reactive Attachment Disorder (RAD).

Children confined to orphanages in some eastern European and other developing countries often suffer from RAD. Instead of connecting with two loving parents, being held, cuddled, and affirmed, infants and toddlers are confined to cribs for most of the day. Jennifer Roback Morse, president and founder of the Ruth Institute, adopted a boy from Romania in 1991. In her book *Love and Economics: Why the Laissez-faire Family Doesn't Work,* she recounts the terrible start in life that her son had. He was fed by a bottle attached to the side of his crib, like a gerbil in a cage. No one picked him up to feed him. No one met his emotional needs. Not surprisingly, he had problems with attachment and a host of behavior issues.

Few people have to deal with that level of dysfunction as infants. This book is not designed to help those with severe psychological issues. I will at times refer to psychology in order to help clarify what it means to trust and lend support to my suggestions for overcoming mistrust. "Grace does not destroy nature, but perfects it," according to St. Thomas Aquinas (*Summa Theologiæ*, I, q. 1, a. 8, ad 2). So we can learn much from those who have studied the workings of the human mind, especially Christian psychologists. But this is essentially a book about living the Christian life more fully, with spiritual suggestions to help my readers mature in their faith. I wrote it for basically healthy people who nonetheless do not trust others and God as they should.

According to the teaching of the Catholic Church, that includes most of us. Everyone who ever sins lacks perfect trust in God. Our mistrust goes back further than Erik Erikson supposed. Besides its psychological roots in our infancy, mistrust has its spiritual roots in the sin of Adam.

Adam passed his mistrust down to us

In the Garden of Eden, Adam and Eve were perfectly happy until the Devil, in the guise of a serpent, sowed seeds of mistrust. God gave man a simple commandment: "Of the tree of the knowledge of good and evil you shall not eat, for in the day that you eat of it you shall die" (Gn 2:17).

The Devil tempted Eve, saying, "You will not die. For God knows that when you eat of it your eyes will be opened, and you will be like God, knowing good and evil" (Gn 3:4–5). So, according to the Devil, God was jealous. He did not want Adam and Eve to be as wise as he was! In her naiveté, Eve swallowed that argument, ate the fruit, and gave some to Adam, who also ate it.

"Then the eyes of both were opened" (verse 6). Their vision changed, but not in the way they had anticipated. Instead of trusting God, they feared him. He was their Creator, their only Father, with whom they had communed daily in the garden. Now they began to look upon him as their Judge. They clung to the idea the Devil had suggested that God was not really good, not really looking out for man's best interests. As the *Catechism of the Catholic Church* puts it:

> Man, tempted by the devil, let his trust in his Creator die in his heart and, abusing his freedom, disobeyed God's command. This is what man's first sin consisted of. All subsequent sin would be disobedience toward God and lack of trust in His goodness. (397)

All of us were born with Original Sin on our souls. Although Baptism washes away Original Sin, our nature is still wounded. We tend to judge God in accordance with our experience of other humans, and if that experience is negative, we might distrust God. We might continue to see God as one who punishes, rather than one who forgives.

Learning not to trust

Fr. Groeschel writes, "No one has had a perfect development, for we are all born into a fallen and wounded world; we will find defects and deficiencies all the way through" (SP 44). Even those of us without serious psychological issues that require counseling can have fixations that hold us back from fully living life as God desires (SP 45).

I can't remember a time when I did not struggle with trust. I do not know exactly what it was in my infancy that set me on the road to distrust. My parents were (and are) loving and conscientious. They are still together after more than fifty years and a few family tragedies of their own. But they were also, like all of us, influenced by the culture in which they lived. My mother followed the parenting advice that was the conventional wisdom of the 1960s: bottle feeding, letting children cry themselves to sleep, and being careful not to spoil them. She believed that crying was a way to give babies needed exercise.

Most child-rearing experts today agree that an infant cannot be spoiled. We cannot bestow too much attention and affection upon him. It is only as children grow older that we must wean them from always having their way. Infants need lots of love. They must know that their needs will always be met.

On the other hand, few mothers have the support of extended family, yet they are expected to be "supermoms," doing everything themselves and doing it perfectly. That's a goal no one can reach. And so, whatever the cause, they make mistakes. Those mistakes often have consequences.

On a Saturday morning when I was five years old, Dad was preparing to take us to my brothers' wrestling practice. Earlier he had dropped off Mom and my sisters Julie and Terri at ballet lessons. I wore my flowered jacket, ready to go. But shortly before we were to leave, I nodded off in a room by myself. When I awoke, the house was quiet. I didn't know how long I had been sleeping.

I ran into the living room where I had left the male members of our family. It was empty. "Dad?" I called. "Dad, are you here?" Silence answered back.

I hurried to the window overlooking the front yard to see if they were still there. The front yard was empty. The driveway was also deserted.

Was it possible that Dad had forgotten me? I knew I should check the rest of the rooms in the house to be sure, but I could not bring myself to walk back down the hall I had just traversed. Instead, I called out one more time, as loudly as my little lungs allowed, "Is anybody home?" There was no answer.

I sank down on a blue plastic chair by the window with my face to the room. I did not want to turn my back on the far corners, which were in shadow. Outside a neighbor's dog barked and I stiffened momentarily. The ticking of the clock on the mantel provided a soothing sound amid the mysterious creaking noises of the house. Every second brought me closer to my family's return. *Dad will notice I'm missing,* I told myself. Or one of my three brothers who were with him would speak up. I kept my jacket on as I waited.

A sudden noise startled me. Was there an intruder in the house? No, it was only a fan somewhere. I took a slow, deep breath.

Little by little as the clock ticked away, the shadows in the corners spread themselves across the shag carpet, inching towards me. I tried not to look at them. Instead, I traced the raised flower pattern on the chair with my finger, and counted the small brass tacks that lined the edges of the seat. Sometimes a car would pass, and I would turn my head hopefully towards the window without turning fully around, only to be disappointed when it continued up or down our hilly street without stopping.

At last I heard a car approach more slowly. Yes, it was turning into the driveway. I listened for it to stop and was relieved. Car doors slammed. Feet sounded on the front steps. By the time the key was in the door, I had jumped down to meet Dad. The door swung open, and we were face to face.

"You forgot me!" I greeted him. My voice was unsteady. "I fell asleep and when I woke up you were gone."

I watched for a sign of sympathy, but his face was unconcerned. "You shouldn't have fallen asleep," he replied. Then John, David, and Joe pushed past him into the room, laughing and talking about the practice. Dad was immediately distracted, and nothing more was said to me.

This was not a major incident, nor surely an uncommon one. It could have happened in almost any family. Other children who were forgotten by their parents may not have minded it as much. Some may have even enjoyed being home alone. What one child will joke about may deeply hurt another. We have different temperaments and unique personalities.

For me, this incident remains etched in my memory when countless others were forgotten. It was easy for my parents to overlook me, a quiet child, the fifth born in six years. I imagine that I was forgotten sometimes before the shadows of my earliest memories as well.

I learned a lesson in those early days of "crying it out" that was confirmed by my father's reaction to leaving me home alone. Sensitive, yet eager to please those in authority, I tried to do what I believed my parents expected. Negative emotions, I thought, should simply be ignored. Sadness, fear, anger, frustration—these were signs of weakness and immaturity. In a home with children being born one after another, we had to grow up quickly. There was no time for us to be treated like babies once a younger sibling arrived.

I learned—whether or not my parents consciously taught such a lesson—that a Christian must not only be good, he must be strong. I was not naturally strong, physically or emotionally. But I began to shut my feelings up inside of me and to equate weakness with unworthiness.

As I grew older, I was never able to stand letting younger siblings "cry it out." Many times I sought to calm them in their cribs. My natural sympathy reached out to soothe others, while my learned stoicism kept others from reaching out to me. But underneath my quiet shell I was hungry for affirmation. I became convinced that I must hide my emotions in order to gain others' respect. I could not trust others to accept the real me.

As Fr. Groeschel points out, some children who have a solid start in life still get "hung up" on trust. Others who have troubled beginnings overcome them and become mature, well-adjusted individuals. I believe that at least some of my siblings did learn to trust.

It is not so much the events of my life—or of Therese's, for that matter—that concern me, but the personalities that were formed through these events. How did we choose to respond to them? What part did they play in our maturing selves?

Who is to blame?

Who is to blame? This is the first in a series of questions that can be the enemies of trust. When we look for someone to blame, we risk seeing ourselves as victims, rather than human beings given free will and the grace of Christ. This in turn can lead to despair. We feel we are helplessly out of control of our lives, that people and circumstances are against us. We fail to recognize and accept responsibility for our sins and mistakes.

This pseudo-paranoia, which pits the whole world against oneself, causes us to close our hearts to others and even to God. Determined not to be hurt or "duped" again, we reject both trust and love.

Adam blamed Eve for his sin. Eve blamed the serpent. And we, their children, blame one another.

My purpose in analyzing my early years is not to lay blame, but to ponder, so that I may grow—and help others to do the same.

Trust requires us to make ourselves vulnerable. It requires us to let go. And the first thing we must let go of is the role of accuser. In the Bible, Accuser is a name for the Devil. In fact, *Satan* means *Accuser* or *Adversary* in Hebrew. The Devil teaches us to blame, just as he taught our first parents. God, on the other hand, forgives. Christ, the new Adam, forgave even those who crucified him.

When we are honest, we must admit that sometimes others have hurt us. Some people are cruel. Others are simply self-centered and indifferent. Still others are well meaning, but ignorant or weak. We cannot fault parents for following the morally neutral parenting customs of their day. Of course, when people have done grievous injury to an infant—who is incapable of either sinning or defending himself—anger can be righteous. But at some point we have to let even our righteous anger go, and the sooner, the better. We will talk more about anger in chapter 7.

When we forgive, those who have harmed us lose their power over us. They no longer determine the outcome of our interactions with new individuals. They no longer limit our capacity for love and trust. We triumph over them and over our baser selves. We also triumph over the Devil.

Consider the attitude of the psalmist who wrote, "I trusted, even when I said . . . 'No man can be trusted '" (Ps 116:10; ICEL translation from the Liturgy of the Hours). He did not let his experience of being betrayed define him. Even though he had found *no one* to be trustworthy, he labored to trust.

This does not mean that we should let others trample on us. Neither does it mean that we should naively trust everyone. Jesus instructed his disciples to be "as wise as serpents and innocent as doves" (Mt 10:16). A healthy person acknowledges when others have failed him. He does not pretend all is well when it is not. At the same time, he acknowledges that only God knows the extent to which others are responsible for their actions. Instead of holding onto anger against others, he uses his pain as a means to grow closer to Christ. He does not blindly trust those who appear to be untrustworthy. But he is willing to risk some heartache for the possibility of loving and being loved, and *he is unafraid.*

Do our early years define us?

The circumstances of each person's infancy are unique. Some people may not be able to identify anything that went wrong in their early years. Others come from a broken home, where one or both parents were absent from the beginning. Some were orphaned or adopted. Others were raised by a single mother or grandparents. Still others lived with both parents, but other stresses in the family interfered with the attention they needed as infants. The death or illness of siblings, unemployment, poverty, domestic abuse, or major character flaws in their parents may have hampered their early growth.

Whatever the case, if we had less than an ideal start in life that led us to have a problem trusting people, it does not have to define our whole life.

Reading Fr. Groeschel's book, I was reminded of my lack of trust—which has been a repeating theme in my life. The book spoke in detail of Erik Erikson's theory. I had previously learned about Erikson in my education studies. Fr. Groeschel noted that those who have learned the wrong lesson in any of Erikson's stages must go back and renegotiate the stage. They must choose the positive outcome this time, if they wish to be psychologically mature individuals.

When I read that, it reminded me of the story of Nicodemus. Nicodemus secretly came to give Jesus his allegiance.

> Jesus answered him, "Truly, truly, I say to you, unless one is born anew, he cannot see the kingdom of God." Nicodemus said to him, "How can a man be born when he is old? Can he enter a second time into his mother's womb and be born?" (Jn 3:3–4)

Can I go back and become an infant again? Of course not. Then how can I renegotiate the trust-versus-mistrust conflict and get it right this time? For a while I searched for internet resources for doing this. But finding nothing helpful, I soon forgot about it. I was busy bearing and raising my own children by this point.

Today, I believe that not only have I found the answer to renegotiating the trust versus mistrust conflict; I have been practicing it. I have not found it in psychology or self-help texts, although they have been of some help. Therese provides the answer.

Therese forged a new path towards sanctity that she called the little way of spiritual childhood. To God, we are and always will be children. Jesus said that spiritual childhood is necessary for salvation. We can renegotiate trust by learning to trust God as our Father. Doing so will free us to be able to trust others as well. It will free us from fear, anxiety, presumption, and despair. It will give us a peace deeper than any we have ever known.

Questions for Reflection

1. Have I struggled with trust all my life? What circumstances in my infancy may have contributed to this?

2. Am I ready to forgive my parents or other caregivers for their mistakes?

3. Do I believe that God is my Father? Do I desire to trust him? Do I think it is possible (with his help)?

Practical Suggestions

* Set aside a specific time daily to pray the Our Father. If you already have a dedicated time for prayer, you can make this a part of it. Say the words slowly, meditating on their meaning. How does each phrase of the prayer relate to trust?

* If you have been estranged from someone who has hurt you, can you find it in your heart to forgive? Sit down and write a heart-felt letter to him or her. Express your hurt and anger in a non-threatening and Christian way. End the letter with an extension of forgiveness. Let the reader know you desire his good, not revenge. Then decide whether it is prudent to send the letter. If not, keep it where you can reread it whenever anger and resentment threaten to return.

Chapter Three
Dealing with Childhood Tragedies

And after you have suffered a little while, the God of all grace, who has called you to his eternal glory in Christ, will himself restore, confirm, strengthen, and establish you.

1 Pet 5:10

Therese spent a few shining, happy years as the darling of her mother, who described her antics in letters to friends and relatives. But it was not long before another tragedy hit the Martin family.

In 1876, Zelie's sister Marie-Louise, now Visitation Sr. Marie-Dosithée, was dying of tuberculosis. Marie-Dosithée's looming death moved Zelie to finally seek advice for her own medical problems. Lack of confidence in the doctors available to her had kept her from doing so in the past. But she had been suffering far more than any of her loved ones knew. Besides the lingering pain in her breast, headaches, eye-strain, and digestive problems also troubled her (SL 23). Shortly before the end of the year, she consulted Dr. Prevost. He diagnosed a "fibrous tumor"—cancer—and told Zelie an operation would be useless. At the urging of her brother and sister-in-law, she sought a second opinion from prominent surgeon Dr. Alphonse-Henri Notta in Lisieux. His conclusion was the same. It was too late to save her life. The best doctors could do was prolong it.

The next several months marked Zelie's deterioration, especially after Marie-Dosithée died in February. A pilgrimage to Lourdes with her three eldest daughters only aggravated her condition. By August of 1877, she was hardly sleeping at all due to pain and fever.

"All the details of my mother's illness are still present to me," Therese wrote nearly twenty years later, "and I recall especially the last two weeks she spent on earth" (SS 33).

The Martins asked Adolphe Leriche and his wife Marie to take in Celine and Therese during the day. Adolphe was Louis' nephew. Years earlier, he had purchased Louis' watch-and-jewelry-making business. The girls addressed their cousin's wife as "Madame Leriche."

"Celine and I were like poor exiles," Therese mourned (ibid.). No one had told the two young girls that their mother was dying, but they knew something was terribly wrong with her. They longed to be near her and the rest of the family. They tried to play with the Leriche children, but they could not focus on their games. They clung to each other for support, deepening a friendship that would be one of the most significant of both their lives.

Madame Leriche did her best for her little cousins. One morning she arrived at the Martin family home so early that they had not had time to say their usual morning prayers. Both girls were upset. On the way to the Leriche home, Celine whispered to Therese, "Should we tell her?"

"Oh, yes!" Therese answered.

Celine, as the bigger sister, tried to be bold. "Madame Leriche, we haven't said our morning prayers."

"Well, my little girls," she replied, "don't worry. You shall say them at our home." Once they arrived, she led them to a large empty room. "You may say your prayers here." Then she left them, closing the door behind her.

Celine and Therese looked at each other in surprise. "This isn't the way Mama does it," said Celine. "She always says our prayers with us." Nonetheless, the two girls did the best they could on their own.

Later, Madame Leriche gave Celine a beautiful, ripe apricot to eat. Celine had other plans. "I will give it to Mama," she said to her sister, tucking it into a pocket. But Zelie was already far too ill to eat the fruit when it was offered to her. (See SS 33.)

On August 26, a priest gave Zelie the Last Rites. By this time, Zelie could no longer speak and her limbs were swollen. Therese wrote, "The touching ceremony of the last anointing is also deeply impressed on my mind. I can still see the spot where I was by Celine's side. All five of us were lined up according to age, and poor Papa was there too, sobbing" (ibid.).

A telegram summoned Isidore and Celine Guerin, Zelie's brother and sister-in-law, from Lisieux. They arrived on August 27. Zelie died shortly after noon the next day, her husband and brother at her side. Therese did not see her mother until the day after her death, when Louis brought her in to give Zelie a last kiss.

"I don't recall having cried very much, neither did I speak to anyone about the feelings I experienced," she wrote (ibid.). But her emotions broke out in other ways. "My happy disposition completely changed after Mama's death. . . . If God had not showered His beneficent *rays* upon His little flower, she could never have accustomed herself to earth for she was too weak to stand up against the rain and the storms" (SS 35, emphasis in the original). Therese became extremely sensitive, crying when she did not get her way or when she made mistakes.

Therese's older sisters stepped in to take a mother's place in her life. Celine and Therese each chose a "second mother" from among their older sisters. Celine decided that Marie, the oldest, would now be her mama. Therese chose Pauline, the next oldest, as her second mother. Therese had always had a special love for Pauline. Now this sister who was so much like their mother in character offered Therese the best substitute she could. She made Therese face her childhood fears and never spoiled her (SS 35).

A childhood loss

Like Therese, many of us have childhood experiences that pose challenges to trust. In this chapter, I'll share one tragedy from my childhood. We'll see how asking *why* tragedy happens can trap us in our pain, and explore what we should ask instead. We'll read how Pauline's departure for the Carmelite convent affected Therese. And we'll consider whether a God who allows suffering can be all good and all powerful.

My childhood was happy, for the most part. But a family tragedy when I was only six subconsciously hindered my trust for decades.

In the early 1970s, my parents became involved in the Catholic Charismatic Renewal. They helped start a prayer group in our small city in southeastern Washington state. Soon afterwards, they decided to drive to an annual Catholic charismatic conference on the campus of the University of Notre Dame. Our family had always enjoyed road trips.

The conference that year was to be held during the second full week of June, ending with Pentecost. My parents planned to begin our family vacation for the summer with a weekend retreat in Spokane, then travel on to South Bend, Indiana, beginning Monday. There were seven children in our family at that time, ranging in age from twelve down to two. Some friends, Mrs. Carlson (not her real name) and her children Andrew and Theresa, accompanied us.

My memories of the retreat are vague. We had been to the Immaculate Heart Retreat House two years previously, after finishing the Nine First Fridays devotion to the Sacred Heart. The two events, along with a later retreat, are blurred in my mind.

The children were divided by age group to have their own retreats. My parents and older siblings went to Reconciliation. We stayed overnight at the retreat center on Sunday.

Monday morning dawned. Our custom was for one of us children to lead the family in prayer for a safe trip. That day, June 10, 1974, no one wanted to volunteer. It was 6 A.M. We were all too tired. At last, my sister Terri agreed to pray. She composed a short prayer to which we added our Amens. She was ten years old.

Then three adults and nine children piled into our green station wagon. I was in the back with the seat down. Siblings Julie (eleven) and David (eight), and Theresa and Andrew Carlson were with me. The flat bed was meant for cargo transport, but it was common for large families to use it for extra seating in those days. This was before the era of seatbelt laws. Even so, my parents had always insisted that everyone be buckled in. With the three extra people in the car, there simply were not enough buckles. It was the first and last time my parents would ever allow us to go without seatbelts.

Behind us an open trailer held our sleeping bags and luggage. It was far from steady. As Dad shut us in, he said, "Keep your eyes on the trailer and tell us if it rocks too much." Then he circled around to the driver's seat. Mom and Mrs. Carlson sat in the front too, my brother Daniel, aged two, on Mom's lap. Terri and two brothers occupied the middle seat.

"Count off," Mom called.

"One," said John.

"Two," said Julie. And each child called out his number in turn. This was our parents' way of checking to see that everyone was in the car.

We started the trip obeying Dad's command about the trailer, but it was boring watching it, especially when the rest of the family was spotting wildlife on the side of the road. Before long we had forgotten all about it.

Just west of Missoula, Montana, we stopped for a picnic lunch. After we ate sandwiches, chips, and brownies, Dad lined us up in front of the car in order of age—with Mom near the driver's door in plaid bell bottoms and dark sunglasses—and took movies. Terri, the third oldest, broke the smoothly descending line with her height. She was as tall as John and "a head" taller than Julie, as Mom liked to say. Then Dad and the Carlson kids joined the group and Mrs. Carlson shot still photos in two different arrangements.

Julie complained that she had been carsick in the back, so she and Terri changed places when we returned to the car. Mrs. Carlson took over the wheel. Those of us in the "way back" lounged on our tummies facing towards the front, coloring or writing in journals. We each had a tiny notebook with a cover photo of a zoo animal, for recording the details of the trip. Mine had a giraffe.

Half an hour after we got back on the road, something fell on the floor in the front seat and Mrs. Carlson bent down to pick it up. She lost control of the car and it swerved. The trailer flipped over, pulling the car after it.

We rolled over three times before landing in the grassy median of Interstate 90.

I've never been able to remember the accident itself. I don't know if my six-year-old mind blacked it out in self-preservation, or if repeatedly bumping my head on the ceiling knocked me out. The first thing I recall is a stinging pain in my left leg. I looked down and saw blood. I was lying on an open sleeping bag in the grass. A brown-haired woman I didn't know was gently washing my wound. Not far behind her was the wreck of our car. I whimpered and she tried to soothe me.

God showed his care for us in so many ways that day. A doctor and two nurses were driving by on the other side of the highway, saw the accident, and pulled over to help. A member of a Pentecostal church my parents sometimes attended (in addition to going to Mass) in our hometown also witnessed it, although we were hours away from home. Countless other strangers made sure we were all out of the car.

Everyone in the middle seat had been properly belted in and was fine. Mom had been dozing in the front. As the car turned upside down, she jerked awake, throwing her hands up in surprise. Daniel flew off her lap. Without even thinking, Dad reached up and caught him by the ankles before he hit the windshield. Daniel later complained of sore feet. He and Joe, the next youngest, came and stood over me as I lay awaiting the arrival of an ambulance. They were laughing and joking, too young to recognize the seriousness of the situation.

The adults were all unharmed.

At last there were sirens and flashing lights. Emergency personnel loaded all of us who had been in the back of the car into the ambulance. They slammed the doors closed behind us. Lying on a stretcher near the left window, I was well enough to be left alone. I didn't stop to think about how the others were doing or what was keeping the emergency workers busy. Instead, I watched the tops of the trees go by as we raced back towards Missoula. Finally the view turned to bricks, and we were pulling up under the covered entrance to the hospital emergency room.

Doctors and nurses surrounded us. They undressed me to my underclothes and examined me for injuries. Then when it was clear the minor cut on my leg was my only problem, someone threw a knotted, white blanket over me. As nurses wheeled me down the hall to an exam room, I felt exposed.

After a time, a doctor came. He sewed up my leg with purple thread.

Later that evening, I was watching TV in my hospital room. Theresa Carlson was asleep in the next bed. She, like many of us, had bumped her head several times and was hospitalized for observation. Mom and Mrs. Carlson came to visit.

"Turn the TV off," Mom said. I pressed the button on the remote, one of the novelties that had brought an element of fun to our ordeal. "Terri didn't make it," Mom said without preface. Her voice was peaceful. I watched her face through the dark blue bars of the hospital crib, as she told me the details. If she had been crying, I could find no trace of it. Terri had been thrown out the rear window, and the tumbling car had crushed her, Mom told me. Dad tried to revive her, but she had most likely died instantly.

My tears began to flow.

"She's happy now," Mom continued. "She's in heaven with Jesus. We shouldn't cry. That's just feeling bad for ourselves, not for her. She can't suffer any more." I nodded and wiped my eyes. Those few tears were the only ones I shed for Terri as a child. If Mom could accept her death, then so could I.

Some adults, when I tell them this story, dismiss my feelings, saying, "You probably didn't understand what was happening. You were only six." And then I am back in that bed with the bars all around me. Placed in a crib at six years old.

A few months earlier, Terri had won a school art contest called "What the Eyes Can See." She had drawn a purple mountain beyond a field of grass and wildflowers. When Mom and Dad looked up from the place where she died, they saw a similar scene. The picture helped them to believe that God's hand was upon Terri and all of us.

When I became a mother myself, I felt the impact of what had happened in a new and disturbing way. Pregnant with our first child, I was seized with sudden terror while driving down the icy Minnesota highway to our apartment. What if the car spun out of control? What if the car behind me refused to drive slowly enough for the weather, and slammed into our van? I was carrying a life totally innocent and totally dependent on me.

I was in tears when I reached home. After that, Dan agreed to drive me to and from work for the rest of the winter.

The danger of asking *why?*

Who is to blame? is the first question that can be an enemy of trust, as we saw earlier. The second question is *why?* It's natural to ask *why* in the face of suffering, especially when children are involved. Why did God let Zelie Martin, a good and holy mother, die, when she had five children to care for, the youngest only four years old? Why didn't he protect my family, on the way from one religious event to another? Why does he let children be abused and neglected?

Holocaust survivor Victor Frankl, author of *Man's Search for Meaning* wrote, "Suffering ceases to be suffering in some way in the moment that it finds a meaning" (Boston: Beacon Press, 2006, 77). We hungrily search for an explanation we can cling to.

St. Paul wrote, "We know that in everything God works for good with those who love him, who are called according to his purpose" (Rom 8:28). The fulfillment of this verse in our lives remains something of a mystery. Suffering can strengthen us and bring us closer to God, but does that mean God causes others to suffer for my spiritual benefit? Surely other people are not pawns in God's plan to make me holy.

God cared for Terri as well as he cares for me. Romans 8:28 was true for her too. It was true for Zelie Martin. It was true for Therese.

Fr. Bernard Bro has suggested that Zelie's faithful and peaceful acceptance of her suffering was the model for Therese in her adult battle with tuberculosis (STL 37). Therese knew how a suffering Christian should act. That was the legacy her mother left her. But, given the choice, surely Therese would have preferred to spare her mother an agonizing death from cancer. Surely for many years she must have wished her mother were still with her!

Would Therese have become a saint if she had never witnessed Zelie's suffering? We simply don't know. We do know that countless people have lost loved ones tragically without becoming saints. Therese found meaning in her loss as she grew older. She learned to accept and embrace it. It became a means of sanctification for her. God worked through it for her good.

I admit I do not understand the ways of God. My mind is too small. And sometimes my heart is too heavy. When tragedy strikes, I find myself among those asking *why?* But as a Christian, I too must believe and embrace St. Paul's words.

After Terri's death, my parents stayed at a rectory overnight while they arranged for her body to be taken home and waited for our release from the hospital. My mother asked the priest why God did not answer Terri's prayer for a safe trip. He replied that perhaps God *did* answer it by bringing Terri safely to heaven. It is no mystery why Romans 8:28 has been one of my father's favorite Bible verses since that time.

If we want suffering to have meaning, *why* is usually the wrong question to ask. In my sister's case, there was an answer to one *why* question that resonated with us. But often there is not. Rabbi Harold Kushner wrote in *When Bad Things Happen to Good People* that asking *why* keeps us focused on the tragedy. We need to move on, because we still have a life to live. The question we should ask, he says, is, "Now that this has happened, what shall I do about it?" (New York: Shocken Books, 1981, 137).

How can I let God use this tragic situation for good in my life? How can I become a better person, more closely united to his will, than I was before it happened? When we ask the question this way, we become part of the answer. We allow God to fulfill his promise in and through us.

Our vision is limited. We cannot see the future. We will never fully know on earth how our personal tragedies and those of our loved ones fit into God's eternal plan for good.

Victor Frankl used this analogy with some of his patients. Suppose researchers seeking to create a polio vaccine repeatedly drew blood from an ape for testing. The ape would be suffering for a noble purpose, the prevention of a serious, debilitating disease. However, being an ape, it would be unable to comprehend the meaning of its suffering. Its mind cannot work that way. But the meaning would still exist.

Or think about the Apostles of Jesus. How did they feel when he died by crucifixion? It must have seemed like the end of everything good. Their highest hopes and dreams were completely crushed. But that was only because they did not yet understand that "the Christ should suffer these things and enter into his glory" (Lk 24:26).

Now, the Apostles (except Thomas) only had to wait three days to learn how wrong they had been. The Crucifixion was actually a new beginning for everything good. Even death cannot triumph over God and his people!

We might have to wait much longer than three days to see God's purpose fulfilled. But the good can begin in our hearts today—if we let God work.

Pauline enters the cloister

In the summer of 1882, Therese overheard Marie and Pauline talking. Pauline had made up her mind to enter the Carmelite monastery in Lisieux. Barely five years had passed since Zelie's death. Therese was less than ten years old. She was devastated once more. As they had with Zelie's decline, the Martin family had kept Pauline's coming departure secret from Therese. Only years later would Pauline realize what a mistake this was (SL 43).

Therese wrote, "I didn't know what Carmel was, but I understood that Pauline was going to leave me to enter a convent. I understood, too, that she *would not wait for me* and that I was going to lose my second *Mother!* Ah! how can I express the anguish of my heart?" (SS 58, emphasis in the original).

Pauline left for Carmel on October 2. From then on, Therese saw her with the rest of the family on weekend visits to the parlor, but she had only a few minutes at the end when she could actually speak with Pauline. The visits harmed her more than helped. Soon she was suffering from headaches, pains in her stomach and side, loss of appetite, and trouble sleeping. She began squabbling with Celine. Marie had taken charge of Therese when Pauline left home. She was overly severe with Therese, who began talking back (SL 45).

During Holy Week 1883, Louis Martin took Marie and Leonie on a pilgrimage to Paris. Celine and Therese stayed with the Guerins. Two incidents there helped spur on Therese's decline. One day she accidentally called her aunt *Mama.* Her little cousin Marie answered, "My Mama is not your Mama. You no longer have one" (SL 46). As though Therese needed to be reminded!

Then on the Easter Vigil, Uncle Isidore took Therese on a walk, tenderly reminiscing about his sister. This was too much for Therese. She did not dare make any sign of pain before her uncle, but inwardly she was in anguish. Since she was too exhausted to go out with the family that evening, Aunt Celine had her dress for bed. Therese began trembling uncontrollably. Blankets and hot water bottles did her no good.

She lay in bed, trying not to think of the mother she had lost, the sister who lived behind the monastery grille, and the father who was hours away. Chills continued to sweep over her. Isidore, who was a pharmacist, watched her with concern. The next day, he decided to call in Dr. Notta, who had diagnosed her mother.

Dr. Notta was confused by Therese's symptoms, but thought them serious. He prescribed wrapping her in cold, wet towels, a popular remedy for pain, fever, and nervousness.

The Guerins sent a telegram to Paris to call home Louis and his older daughters.

Therese meanwhile began hallucinating and having violent convulsions several times a day (SL 46). She saw her aunt and cousin Jeanne attending her and knew who they were, but when she tried to speak to them, her words were unintelligible. Anxiety seized her.

By the time Louis arrived, Therese was too ill to be moved home to Les Buissonnets in Lisieux, where they had moved shortly after Zelie's death. Instead Celine Guerin and Marie Martin took turns watching over her at the Guerins' home.

Pauline's clothing as a Carmelite was scheduled for April 6. On that day, she would be dressed in the Carmelite habit for the first time, as she entered the novitiate. Everyone avoided speaking about Pauline in Therese's presence, but Therese was determined to attend the event. "I shall go and see Pauline clothed," she repeated ceaselessly.

The morning of April 6, seizures shook her body, but then she suddenly became calm. Insisting she was cured, she persuaded her father to let her see Pauline in the cloister parlor after the ceremony, although he did not allow her to go to the clothing itself. She sat on Pauline's lap and covered her with kisses (SL 62).

After returning to Les Buissonnets, her family insisted she go to bed in Marie's room. Therese said again, "I am perfectly cured." But the next morning she was worse than ever. At times she could neither move nor cry out, even though she remained conscious of everything that went on around her.

Dr. Notta was still unable to make a diagnosis, but confirmed the illness was real, not just a psychological phenomenon.

The Carmelites joined the Martin family in offering prayers and Masses for Therese's healing. The Martins had a favorite statue of Our Lady of Victories. They moved it into Marie's bedroom. Meanwhile, a novena went out to Our Lady of Victories, to whom a famous church in Paris was dedicated.

When letters arrived from Pauline, Therese heard them read with perfect composure and peace. In between, her suffering continued.

Then Therese had a new pain. She discovered that Uncle Isidore suspected she was making herself sick over sorrow at losing Pauline. Therese was consumed with guilt, which would last for five years. Was this all her doing? Was she at fault, bringing herself to the brink of death with her oversensitivity?

On Pentecost Sunday, Leonie was alone in the room with Therese. "Mama, Mama, Mama," Therese called without a break. Was she calling Marie, or mourning the loss of Zelie and Pauline? Leonie did not call their older sister. This was not the first time in her illness that Therese had acted this way. Finally her cries grew louder and Marie came, bringing Celine with her. But, as though she could not see her "third mother" bending over her, Therese continued to cry out. The three sisters were frightened and all knelt at the foot of her bed to pray.

Marie turned and addressed her prayers to the statue of our Lady of Victories. In agony, Therese followed her lead, silently pleading for the Virgin's aid. All at once a "ravishing" smile lit the statue's face (SL 65), visible only to Therese. Therese's pain disappeared at once, as two tears rolled down her cheeks. She was completely cured.

Later in life Therese would believe that her illness was the work of the Devil. Some modern psychiatric experts believe she suffered from a form of Post Traumatic Distress Syndrome. (See, for example, the detailed analysis from the Archives of the Lisieux Carmel online at www.archives-carmel-lisieux.fr.) I see no reason why both explanations cannot be right. The Devil could have used Therese's psychological distress to bring her to the point of utter helplessness. Perhaps, as she would come to believe, he already realized what harm she would do to him. After all, she had dreamed that demons were frightened of her! This spiritual aspect of her illness explains why the Blessed Virgin Mary's intervention was necessary.

We might think this illness would have had a cathartic effect, that from now on Therese would no longer be emotionally impaired from her mother's death. But two minor setbacks in her health when Leonie would not give Therese her way made the family afraid to oppose her. Instead they spoiled her. They let her have her way in everything. She retained her extreme sensitivity, crying easily whenever someone criticized her. She remained a small child emotionally for many years.

On the other hand, she had the ability to focus on what was really important in life, something we would expect from a mature adult. Her repeated losses taught her to put little stock in passing things. She gave first place to love.

For the next few years, life ran more smoothly in the Martin home. Then Marie joined Pauline in the Carmelite cloister when Therese was fourteen. Once more Therese had lost a mother figure. She suffered a temporary relapse, although much less serious than before. She was learning that God is the only constant in life, the only One we can always depend on never to fail us.

Believing in God's goodness

Sometimes it's hard to believe in the goodness of God when tragedy strikes. At the liberal Lutheran college I attended, the college president once gave an address on the problem of evil. He professed that suffering could not exist in a world where God was both all good and all powerful. If God had power over evil, and he was truly good, he would not allow good people to suffer, the argument went.

So, there were two alternatives. The first was that God was all powerful, but not all good. The president dismissed this. The other alternative was that God was all good, but he had limited power over evil. He embraced this conclusion. Thus, God wanted to protect us from suffering, but was unable to do so.

Over the years I have learned that many other Christians hold this belief. Of course, it completely contradicts Scripture, Sacred Tradition, and the teachings of the Catholic Church. Besides that, it makes no logical sense. If God is less powerful than evil, then evil must really be the ruling force behind the universe. In other words, evil itself must be "god." The implication is anything but comforting. That's ironic, since this teaching was formulated as a response to people's grief and anger, to bring them some sort of peace.

We don't need to teach error to make people feel more comfortable. Ignoring 2,000 years of church teaching leaves room for all kinds of terrible mistakes, like this frightening one. We have to accept the fact that God's ways are beyond the capacity of the human mind to comprehend. We need to make *ourselves* little, not speculate that *God* is.

Having said that, I believe we still can have some insight into the problem of evil. How could God give us free will without also making the suffering of the innocent a possibility? Free will means we can choose to accept or refuse the good. By refusing the good, we choose evil. Choosing evil means causing suffering.

Why did God bother to give us free will, we might ask, if he knew we would sin? Without free will, love cannot exist. Love is not an instinct or a mere pleasurable experience. Love is a choice. Without free will we would be base animals, living by instinct, incapable of true happiness. Heroic acts of self-sacrifice would be impossible. Our life would have no more meaning than the ape's we spoke of earlier.

God saw a better way. Knowing that we would sin, he planned from the beginning to send his Son to redeem and transform us. Christ makes our life meaningful. God used the very thing that most scandalizes us—the suffering of the innocent, in the Person of Jesus—to erase the effects of our bad choices. And by Christ's Death and Resurrection, he did even more than that. He made us his children through Baptism. The life of God lives in us, transforming us. As we unite our suffering with the suffering of Christ, we participate in the redemption of the world.

Again, this is a mystery we will never fully understand until we see God in heaven. But it is a vital part of our faith. God is all good. He wants only good things for us. The more we entrust ourselves to him, the more even our suffering becomes a means of grace for ourselves and for sinners everywhere.

Let us not give in to the lie of Satan that God is evil. Let us not give in to the lie of the world that God is helpless. Despite the reality of evil, we can truly trust God, because he is all good and all powerful.

Questions for Reflection

1. What tragedies have I experienced? How did they affect my faith and trust in God?

2. Do I believe that God can work good out of evil? Am I willing to be part of that good?

3. How might my experiences bring comfort and encouragement to others?

4. Do I acknowledge my littleness before God, knowing that I cannot begin to fathom the depths of his ways?

Practical Suggestions

* In your prayer time, meditate on the Crucifixion. Picture yourself as one of the Apostles. What are your thoughts and feelings? Now imagine seeing Jesus appear on Easter morning. How does everything change for you? Praise God the Father for his generosity and faithfulness in sending his Son to die for us and raising him from the dead.

* Research some saints who have experienced great suffering in their lives. You might try St. Gemma Gilgani, patroness of those suffering from back pain or spinal injuries; St. Peregrine, patron of cancer patients; St. Elizabeth Ann Seton, patroness of those who have lost parents or children; or another saint that speaks to the suffering you have experienced. Invoke his or her help every morning.

Chapter Four
Human Fathers and God the Father

It was I who taught Ephraim to walk; I took them up in my arms.

Hos 11:3

Therese stretched and blinked open her eyes. Morning sun was already streaming in through the bedroom window. But it was Sunday, and she was permitted to sleep in.

Two quick knocks were followed by the door opening, and Pauline entered with some hot chocolate. "Are you awake, sleepy-head?" she asked.

"Good morning, Mama." Therese adjusted her pillow and sat up, as Pauline handed her the warm cup.

Sunday was Therese's favorite day of the week at Les Buissonnets.

When she had finished her chocolate, she slid out of bed, wide awake now. Pauline knelt beside her on the tiled floor to say morning prayers. Then she dressed her for Mass.

Soon Marie took Pauline's place. Come to curl Therese's long, golden hair, her hands were not always gentle. "Ouch! Marie, you're hurting me," Therese cried.

"Oh, what a baby you are. Do you want to look your best for Our Lord at Mass, or not?" Marie asked. Therese was silent.

Skipping down the stairs a few minutes later, she found her father waiting for her. "Ah, good morning, my little Queen," he greeted her. He took her hand and kissed her cheek tenderly.

They held hands all the way to the Cathedral of Lisieux, where Uncle Isidore was church warden. They did not let go until they had found seats next to each other in "the body of the church" (SS 41). Friends and strangers alike smiled and made room for them.

Usually very shy since her mother's death, Therese did not mind the looks of fellow Mass-goers. She focused her attention on listening. Fr. Ducellier wrote good sermons, but his voice was husky and she usually found it difficult to understand his message (SL 34). This day he began talking about the Passion of Jesus. A smile lit Therese's face. For the first time, the preaching made sense!

Still, her eyes strayed to her father's handsome face. Tears welled up and threatened to spill onto his cheeks. Surprised, Therese turned back to the priest and tried to listen more closely. If Papa was on the verge of crying, she too would let the sermon touch her heart.

After Mass, Pauline and Marie went to the Guerins' house for the rest of the day, while Louis and his younger daughters walked back home, Therese again hand-in-hand with her "King." Sometimes she would accompany one of her sisters to the Guerins', but she always feared that Uncle Isidore would ask her questions. She would rather hide in a corner and listen to conversation unnoticed—or, better yet, stay with Papa.

In the evening after supper, Louis, Leonie, Celine, and Therese sat before the blazing fireplace and took turns playing checkers. Then Louis set the youngest two on his knees and sang traditional hymns and anthems, his voice deep, strong, and beautiful.

When the older daughters returned home after sunset, Pauline read aloud to the family from *The Liturgical Year* by Dom Gueranger. She was the teacher of the family since Zelie's death, especially of Celine and Therese.

Sadness crept over Therese as the light faded. Their lovely day was almost gone. Tomorrow she must be back to her lessons. How she wished it could always be Sunday, or some other feast day!

Finally, the family knelt together to pray Night Prayer with Therese at her father's side. A talented mimic, she watched his every gesture, copying even his tone of voice—always with due respect. Then each daughter kissed him, starting with Marie and ending with Therese. Louis grasped her by the elbows and kissed both her cheeks.

"Good night, Papa," she said. "Good night and sleep well" (SS 43).

Father of a saint

Louis was Therese's pre-eminent example of God's fatherhood. This chapter explores the influence our fathers have had on our concept of God. We'll see how Louis parented his daughters, especially after Zelie died. I'll share another tragic memory, this one from my high school years, which drastically changed my relationship with my dad. We'll learn how parenting styles may affect children, for good or for evil. We'll end with one of the few supernatural events in Therese's life—her vision of her father's future suffering.

Although quiet and retiring by nature, Louis embraced the noise and bustle of a household of daughters. He had pet names for all of his girls. Besides his little Queen, Marie was "the diamond," Pauline was "the fine pearl," Leonie was "the good hearted," and Celine was "the bold one" (HF 42).

Opinions of Louis' character differ widely among sources. One author states that Louis was overly sensitive and sometimes moody, and that Therese picked up these characteristics from him. Ida Friederike Gorres suggests that his daughters were always trying to spare his feelings, afraid of upsetting him (ibid.). I have not found convincing evidence of this in other sources. When Therese felt the call to enter Carmel as soon as possible at age fourteen, she was reluctant to tell her father. Gorres cites this as evidence for Louis' fragility. Surely it is understandable that a man who had lost four children at young ages, then his beloved wife, would struggle with himself when his remaining children left him, one by one, to enter convents! Therese's reluctance was natural under the circumstances.

Yes, Louis Martin was easily moved to tears. He suffered loss throughout his life. In addition to his losing his wife and four children, his mother died during Therese's illness in 1883. His father had died nearly twenty years earlier. He may have been more openly sensitive than the average man of his time, but I don't believe he would have had that reputation in our age.

In some ways, Louis tended toward formality and severity. In fact, Gorres also notes that Marie hid his books of writing by the desert fathers, out of fear he would go too far in his asceticism (HF 42). Is this evidence of his fragility or of his toughness on himself? When the older Martin girls were little, he wanted them to use the formal *vous* verb forms when speaking to their parents. Zelie persuaded him to allow all family members to address each other with the familiar *tu*, which was customary (TF).

After Zelie's death, Louis' reserve and reclusiveness isolated the girls from the outside world. He had left some friends behind in Alençon whom he sometimes visited on his own, but he did not know many people in Lisieux and did not go out of his way to make new friends. He may have been concerned about the worldly influence others would exert on his children (ibid.).

Living in the aftermath of the French Revolution and the Napoleonic wars, the Catholics of Therese's day believed the larger culture promoted immorality and godlessness. They kept to themselves, doing little socializing outside their family circles. They developed a subculture. There were often violent outbursts against Catholics and a pervasive anticlericalism. People talked of potential martyrdom (EW 17), although exaggeration was part of the culture of the day as well.

Thus the Martin family was closely knit. Therese's sisters were always her closest companions, with cousins holding the next place, especially after the family moved to Les Buissonnets. This family closeness made it particularly hard for Therese to bear the losses she experienced.

Louis' role in her life was also all the more important. For the first decade that the Martins lived in Lisieux, Louis and Isidore were virtually the only men in Therese's life (SL 33). That changed a bit in 1878, when some of the Guerin's relatives were added to the family circle. We have seen that Therese was somewhat frightened of her uncle. He was coguardian of the Martin girls with their father after Zelie died. But her father's gentleness always attracted her.

Therese could not endure the thought that her father might die as her mother had done (SL 35).

The Martin family's former maid testified during the canonization process, "M. Martin was an excellent father, and he educated his children, all of whom he loved very much, with the greatest care. The Servant of God, Therese . . . was the object of his special affection, but this did not lessen in any way the serious tone of his education of her. He would not tolerate any fault in her. Without being severe, he raised his children in fidelity to all their duties" (TF).

And yet, even when Therese was a toddler, Zelie wrote in a letter that Louis did everything little Therese wanted (SL 18).

Louis used to take Therese on walks after her morning lessons during the week. When Pauline became her teacher, she wanted to discipline Therese when she performed poorly by taking these walks away. However, Louis would not allow this. He cherished this time with his youngest daughter as much as she did. The two of them often stopped in at their parish church to pray, and Louis would buy a small present for Therese afterwards. In the summer, they went on fishing trips together in the surrounding countryside (SL 34). Celine accompanied them on at least some of these fishing expeditions.

In his insistence on these walks and his instructions to Marie to keep curling Therese's hair as she grew older, we can see how he pampered her. He was reluctant to let his little girl grow up. At the same time, he insisted on obedience, respect, and charity. Neither he nor Pauline and Marie tolerated defiance or deceit. Even very little girls must follow God's laws.

Louis himself conscientiously followed the teachings of the Church. "He never opened his shop on a Sunday, and this might have caused him to lose good business. Weekday Masses, nightly adoration, pilgrimages, this man was not ashamed to live as a Christian" (SL 9). In this he was more observant than the average Catholic man of his place and time (HF 47). "My husband is a saintly man," Zelie wrote in a letter, "I wish all women had husbands like him" (SL 13).

According to Marie, Louis once said, "My children, fear nothing for me; I am a friend of God" (HF 42).

Fr. Bernard Bro writes, "It is evident that Therese owed her image of God in large part to the intelligent, strong, and knowing tenderness, ever-present but without indulgence, that her father had for her and that she had for her father" (STL 41). I think there was some indulgence, but only in innocent matters. Otherwise, I find this an apt assessment.

The great love and affection between the two could not cancel out the sorrow each experienced, but it did help them find peace and joy. Just as her father never withheld from her what she asked of him, Therese grew to believe that God could not resist bestowing gifts on those who love and trust him. Her father treated her as a small child until she was fourteen years old. She wished to always remain a small child in relationship to God.

We can also see the influence of Louis' personal piety on Therese's spirituality. Like him, she was drawn to mortification. She learned to embrace her suffering and even to desire to suffer more, that she might offer her suffering to Jesus in love. Like her father, she believed the Lord would always take care of her.

One dad, two types of fathers

My relationship with my father took a sudden turn shortly after my seventeenth birthday. It was a blustery, rainy Thursday evening. Dad was late coming home from work, so Mom asked me to serve my youngest siblings their dinner. As I was scooping fish sticks and oven fries onto their plates, the phone rang.

"Can you get that?" asked Mom, who was busy elsewhere.

I put down the spatula and obeyed. "Is your mom there?" a woman's voice asked.

"May I ask who's calling?" Caller I.D. and do-not-call lists did not exist. We were at the mercy of telemarketers during the dinner hour.

"Just get your mom," she replied.

I shrugged and covered the receiver with my hand. "It's for you, Mom," I called, adding as she approached, "I think it's a salesperson. She wouldn't tell me who she was."

Mom took the phone and I returned to dishing up dinner. I was not really listening, until I heard her ask, "Are you sure you have the right John Wright?" Her voice was tense. I put my hands on the edge of our round dining table and listened. Before the conversation ended, I had turned to face Mom. She had one hand on her heart. My brothers and sister joked with one another, oblivious to what was happening.

"That was a nurse at St. Paul-Ramsey Hospital," Mom said as she hung up the phone. "Dad was in a car accident. He was hit head-on on the way home from work. He's unconscious in Intensive Care. I need to get over there as fast as I can."

We said a quick prayer.

The nurse had advised Mom not to try and drive herself to the hospital because of her anxiety. She should get a friend to bring her. So Mom made several phone calls. First, to my sister Julie, who no longer lived at home. Then to a neighbor named Betty who was in her women's group. This friend called other women in the group and the prayer chain of the Catholic charismatic community that we belonged to. Then she picked Mom up and drove her to the hospital, leaving me in charge.

I served myself dinner. While we ate, the fan of our fourteen-year-old refrigerator rattled and clanged in the background. The appliance had survived the move from Washington to Minneapolis seven years ago. Now we wondered if it was beyond repair. It should have been looked at earlier that day, but the repairman was late with other jobs. The noise provided a strange backdrop to an evening that seemed unreal.

Julie arrived, and we discussed again the few details we knew about the accident. Then I cleared the table and together we did the dishes.

Before long, another community member dropped by. Leone was the kindergarten teacher at our parish school. She knew our youngest siblings well, and volunteered to watch the three who were eight and under so that Julie and I could go to the hospital.

Driving conditions were bad that evening. Rain obscured our vision. Traffic was slow and the roads were slick. Julie drove with extra caution.

We arrived safely at the hospital, and rode the elevator to the intensive care unit. Mom and Betty sat in a waiting room. They were glad to see us.

I'll never forget the sight of Dad when we were allowed in. His skin was bleach-white, eerily unhuman. A maze of tubes surrounded him. Julie gave voice to my thoughts, "That's not my dad." I had believed nothing could get the better of him. Would he ever be the same again? How could we manage without him?

After only a moment a nurse whisked us back out into the waiting room.

I sat on the floor and worked on a 500-piece puzzle, while we waited for the doctor to come and speak with us. In the meantime, my brothers Joe and John arrived. Soon other members of our community came to support us.

Little by little, we learned more details. Dad had been driving on Shepard Road, an undivided, four-lane frontage road on the Mississippi River that was notorious for accidents. A woman driving the other direction crossed the center line and ran into Dad head-on. She was unhurt. The impact pushed the hood and everything under it against Dad's knees, injuring one leg. But his head bore the worst injury. The plastic molding strip around his door broke, and one end smashed into his temple. It took an hour for rescue workers to extract him from the mangled mess.

Within days of the accident, a cartoon in the Minneapolis Star/Tribune would call for changes to make Shepard Road safer.

A doctor finally visited us in the waiting room with the prognosis. "The first forty-eight hours are the most critical. If he wakes up soon, that's a good sign," he said. "An eighteen-year-old brain would likely recover completely. But a forty-five-year-old one . . . We just don't know. And we won't know until he's conscious exactly how his brain was affected." He went on to explain how injuries to different areas of the brain would cause different difficulties and dysfunctions.

Dad did not recover consciousness in those forty-eight hours. In fact, he remained in a coma for six days. I picture those days as long, wintry, and dark—although I know this is a trick of memory. It was only mid-October, in an autumn that was not particularly cold for Minnesota.

Piles of rain-sodden leaves lined the boulevard. But in my mind, the sting of sub-zero temperatures was in the air.

We prayed fervently for his recovery, having no idea what the future would bring. Knowing that hundreds of our fellow Christians were praying with us gave us hope.

When Dad at last awoke, he had forgotten nearly everything—his name, how to feed himself, and even some vocabulary. His mind was often unable to settle on the correct word, so he substituted nonsense syllables in the middle of a sentence. Sometimes he trailed off into complete incoherence.

The first thing he remembered was Mom. He called her Flossy—a nickname she had always detested and he had never used—along with her maiden name. Thinking he was only nineteen, he was shocked when she told him he was middle aged with nine living children.

Not long after he regained consciousness, and before I had been in to visit him again, Mom called me from the hospital where she sat with him most of every day. She put Dad on the phone. I was struck by his voice, weak and crackly like an old man's. After greeting me, Dad seemed to speak randomly. It was a surreal conversation. I expected rationality and heard gibberish instead.

Dad went on to spend six weeks in the hospital. Before being released, he was allowed to visit us for Thanksgiving. While we kids were at Mass, Mom showed him around the house. "Do I really live here?" he asked repeatedly. Everything was strange to him.

After his return home, he was a day patient at the Sister Kenney Institute at Abbott Northwestern Hospital in Minneapolis. Every day he spent hours in therapy, eventually learning to take the bus to and from the hospital by himself.

Now, thirty years later, he still has short-term memory problems that have kept him from ever working again. He could never live alone, although he functions adequately with Mom's help. Some aspects of his personality changed dramatically.

When I was growing up, Dad was the authority figure in the family. He was the bread-winner and primary disciplinarian. His bold, speak-your-mind character contrasted with my quiet reserve and sensitivity for others' feelings. I don't know how it happened, but I became afraid of him. I avoided one-on-one conversations with him, especially about important matters. I envied people who saw their father as *Daddy*, even into the teen years. I had never had a relationship with my dad like that.

In the months before his car accident, Dad had been reaching out to me more. He took me to visit his office, and I actually enjoyed the time alone with him. New possibilities for our relationship were opening up. They were slammed shut with his head injury.

I was a junior in high school when the accident happened. I needed a father's advice about applying for colleges and scholarships. Instead, I had a dad who often forgot my name, struggled to communicate, and was unable to drive (although he did eventually get his driver's license back).

Mom, understandably, had a hard time adjusting. She leaned on me for support more than was good for me. I listened to her complaints and frustrations and found that all my respect for Dad had disappeared with my fear of him.

Temperamentally, he was now apt to let Mom take care of everything. He had changed from a leadership to a hands-off personality. He was more like a teen than an adult. Dad was thrust into a type of spiritual childhood without his consent.

Younger siblings acted out or disrespected Mom in front of him in order to get a reaction. Usually, there was none of substance. But sometimes, he would burst out in an unexpected rage.

At the same time, Dad treated me as his marked favorite. I did not appreciate this. Brothers and one sister blamed me for a situation I had done nothing to bring about and could not change. I wished he would have forgotten me more often. This favoritism fueled the acting out and caused rifts between some family members that have still not healed.

Today, I have a better relationship with Dad than ever. But my view of God has had to undergo many adjustments as I try to understand his true character. Is God someone I should fear? Can I really be open to him without facing rejection or misunderstanding? Or is God a hands-off Father who will watch me make mistakes without interfering? And how should I respond to God and others? Should I seek to be always in charge, or sit back and let others act? This has been my constant challenge.

Authoritarian and permissive fathers

In 1966, psychologist Diana Baumrind observed three different parenting styles and their effects on children. She found that children of authoritarian parents are likely to be anxious and withdrawn. Authoritarian parents are demanding and strict without being warm or understanding. Rules come before relationships. They want little or no input from the child. Their daughters are likely to give up in the face of frustrations, and their sons are likely to exhibit hostility. On the positive side, their children are less likely to join gangs, or abuse drugs or alcohol, and more likely to do well in school than children of permissive parents.

Children of permissive parents often have little control over their emotions, give up easily when confronted with difficult tasks, can be rebellious and defiant, and exhibit various anti-social behaviors.

The ideal parents are authoritative. They have reasonable rules and standards, along with lots of affection for each other and their children. They are firm, but loving. They praise their children for their talents and good behavior. They sometimes, when appropriate, explain the reasons behind their decisions to their children. They might occasionally let the child help choose an appropriate punishment for bad behavior.

Although they over-simplified parenting styles, Baumrind's findings remain influential in psychological circles. She did not include uninvolved parents in her study. Subsequent psychologists have found this category to be worse than either authoritarian or permissive parents. Children of uninvolved parents tend to lack self-control, have low self-esteem, and achieve less academic success.

The U.S. Department of Health and Human Services notes,

> Even from birth, children who have an involved father are more likely to be emotionally secure, be confident to explore their surroundings, and, as they grow older, have better social connections with peers. . . .
>
> The way fathers play with their children also has an important impact on a child's emotional and social development. Fathers spend a much higher percentage of their one-on-one interaction with infants and preschoolers in stimulating, playful activity than do mothers. From these interactions, children learn how to regulate their feelings and behavior. Rough-housing with dad, for example, can teach children how to deal with aggressive impulses and physical contact without losing control of their emotions. (*The Importance of Fathers in the Development of Healthy Children*, 2006, 12, 13)

Generally speaking, an infant's relationship with his mother is primary in the first two years of life, when Erik Erikson's trust-versus-mistrust conflict is being worked out (see chapter 2). But as the child begins interacting more with others, his relationship with his father grows in importance. Dads begin to model what manhood and fatherhood mean.

In the United States today, there is an epidemic of uninvolved fatherhood. According to the 2010 federal census, one out of three children lives in a household that does not include his biological father. Many Americans do not have a good model of God's fatherhood in their lives.

We also know that our culture tends to see God as *non-judgmental*—an indulgent parent who doesn't like to mention the word *sin*. Perhaps these two phenomena are related.

People who grew up with authoritarian fathers might view God as a tyrant. The new atheists, such as the late Christopher Hitchens, often have this view of God's character. Catholic psychologist Dr. Paul Vitz has written a book titled *Faith of the Fatherless: a Psychology of Atheism.* As a former atheist himself, he proposes that some of recent history's most vocal and tyrannical atheists were reacting to the absence of a good father figure in their lives.

Again I emphasize that we are not looking for someone to blame when we examine our relationships with our fathers. But if we have consistent trouble trusting God, it helps us to consider the roots of the problem. We may need to come to terms with our parents' shortcomings.

We can choose not to let these shortcomings continue to hamper our relationship with God. God is a father, but human fathers are not God! We need to learn that God will always be there for us, even if at times our human fathers were not.

God is not authoritarian, permissive, or neglectful. He is firm but loving. He does not overlook our sin, but he forgives us when we repent. We need never be afraid to approach him and ask for his mercy.

Therese's vision of her father

In the summer of 1879 or 1880, Louis Martin took a business trip to Alençon. One day during his absence, Therese was by herself in an attic room at Les Buissonnets, looking out the window into the afternoon sunshine. She gazed with joy on the garden below. Nature seemed to dance in jubilation.

Suddenly, a man appeared by the laundry building. He was dressed just as Louis would have been, and was about the same height, only he stooped as he walked the length of the garden. His face was covered with a dark cloth. Therese shivered. Papa was not expected back for two days. Was she seeing a ghost?

Don't be silly, she chided herself. *Of course it's Papa. He's come home early, that's all. Why is he so bent over? And why is he hiding his face?* "Papa! Papa!" she called out the window. Her voice was trembling.

The man kept walking, as though he had not heard her. He disappeared behind a row of trees that divided the path and never reappeared on the other side of them.

Marie and Pauline had heard Therese calling in the next room, and Marie ran to see what the matter was. "Papa is still in Alençon," she said. "Why are you calling him?"

In a frightened voice, Therese told her what she had seen.

Marie laid her hand on Therese's shoulder. "Don't worry, little one. I'm sure it was only Victoire. You know how she loves to play tricks on you. She has put an apron on her head to frighten you. You'll see. Come, let's go and find her."

Pauline joined them in the corridor. The sisters found their servant Victoire in the kitchen, dressed normally, and attending to her duties. She protested strongly that she had not been outdoors.

"It wasn't Victoire," said Therese. "I know it wasn't. It was a man. He looked exactly like Papa."

"Let's look in the trees to see if someone's hiding there," Marie suggested. Therese nodded silently.

There was no one near the grove where Therese had seen the man disappear, and no sign that anyone had been there recently.

"You must have been dreaming, Therese," said Pauline. "Maybe you dozed off sitting at the window. Try to forget it."

But Therese could not forget it. Not then, not for the rest of her life. As time went on, she became convinced she had seen a vision of her father's future.

Besides the miraculous cure at age ten, this was one of the few supernatural events in Therese's life. She saw no more visions. She never performed a miracle or experienced locutions. She did have a few dreams in adulthood that may have been supernatural in nature, assuring her she was on the right path. But most of her life was devoid of mystical experiences.

Perhaps this vision was God's way of preparing her for the suffering her father would endure after she entered the cloister. Her greatest fear—losing her father—was going to take place. By giving her this vision, God showed her that he was in control of Louis' health and life. God knew what Louis would have to undergo. It was not outside his providence. All the Martin sisters would later be comforted by this knowledge.

Questions for Reflection

1. Was my father uninvolved, permissive, authoritarian, authoritative, or a combination of these? Did I have other father figures who better represented God to me?

2. How might my relationship with my father have affected my image of God?

3. Have I forgiven him for any mistakes he made? Am I willing to take responsibility for the way I view God from here on?

Practical Suggestions

* If you are interested in learning how God fathered his people Israel throughout the Old Testament, try reading *A Father Who Keeps His Promises* by Scott Hahn.

* Jesus said, "I and the Father are one" (Jn 10:30). Make a list of the ways in which Jesus acted as an ideal father towards his disciples. How was he firm? How was he loving and forgiving? How did he show himself to be trustworthy? Now use these insights to meditate on how he might counsel you in your present circumstances.

Chapter Five
Becoming an Adult While Remaining a Child

Be babes in evil, but in thinking be mature.

1 Cor 14:20

Therese celebrated her first Communion in 1884, following a retreat and lengthy preparation at the Benedictine school where she was a day student. The students had to obtain permission from the school's chaplain every subsequent time they wanted to receive the Sacrament. Therese received Jesus several times during that year, including once just two weeks after her original Communion (SL 53). Apparently, this was unusual. Most of the other girls were not permitted to return to Communion for an entire year, as was the custom.

In May 1885, they prepared for the "second Communion" (SL 55). The preparation and celebration were almost as intense as the year before.

The France of Therese's day was still influenced by Jansenism, a heresy which had arisen in the seventeenth century. In some ways akin to Calvinism, Jansenism taught (among other things) that man should fear God and tremble before him. Even two centuries later, long after the Church had condemned Jansenism, "fire and brimstone" sermons were common. Catholic priests in France commonly discouraged their parishioners from receiving the Eucharist frequently, because they were unworthy.

Abbé Domin was the school chaplain, and, thus, Therese's confessor. In 1884 he warned the girls preparing for first Communion about the dangers of making a sacrilegious Communion and the reality of hell (SL 51). For the retreat before the "second Communion," Therese got out the notebook she had used a year earlier and added to her notes. She wrote, "What Monsieur the Abbé told us is very frightening. He spoke to us about mortal sin" (SL 55).

Therese listened to his preaching with growing alarm. Doubts assailed her. How could she be sure she was not on the road to hell? How did she know she was in a state of grace? Maybe she had committed some terrible sin and was too proud to admit it! She recalled her every minor fault. Sin and shame seemed to lurk everywhere.

Therese could not confide in any of her teachers, and she had no private conversations with Pauline any more. So one morning, while Marie was curling Therese's hair, Therese poured out her heart. She told Marie everything she could think of that she had done wrong, including passing critical thoughts about Marie herself. This became a ritual, with Therese in tears each morning as Marie acted as her confessor, telling her in turn what she should confess to a priest and what she should forget. Always practical, Marie let her confess only a few sins at a time. This troubled Therese until Marie offered to carry the rest of Therese's faults herself. Then Therese experienced a fleeting peace.

Therese would later call her eighteen-month trial with scruples a martyrdom (SS 84). Headaches plagued her. When Celine graduated from the school, leaving her with no confidant there, Therese found herself too consumed with emotional and physical distresses to continue attending. She came home to finish her education under a tutor.

In October 1886, Marie unexpectedly joined Pauline in the cloister. Unlike Pauline, who had long expressed a call to religious life, Marie had difficulty choosing a vocation. Neither the convent nor marriage attracted her. She made up her mind at age twenty-six. After her decision, she entered Carmel in a matter of weeks.

Therese's scruples were still raging. To whom could she turn now?

She had resisted the rigidity of the religion of her culture as well as a sensitive child bereft of her mother could. She wanted to believe in the mercy of God. But she was not strong enough to stand against the harsh teachings of the day. Her struggle against scruples was one of the most difficult of her life.

Pauline and Marie had each in turn done their best for her. But other family members provided what she truly needed. Four little siblings of hers were in heaven with Jesus. She later recalled, "I spoke to them with the simplicity of a child, pointing out that, as the youngest in the family, I had always been the most loved, the one who had been showered with my sisters' tender care." They too were obligated to show her special love, she argued (SS 93).

Almost immediately, the "holy innocents" of the family proved their love. They interceded for her before God's throne, winning her a grace that saved her. Her scruples disappeared and peace flooded her heart. Perhaps their littleness influenced her developing spirituality. She began learning how to trust God like a little child.

Childlike, but not childish

In the spiritual life, we must distinguish childlikeness from childishness. This chapter will demonstrate the danger of counting our merits before God. We'll find that even good devotions can hinder our spiritual growth, if we rely on them too much. I will share the trials of being a new parent, which began to teach me humility. We'll consider a third question that can bar the way to trust. Then we'll see how Therese grew up, finally overcoming the sensitivity that had plagued her since her mother's death.

Therese's budding understanding of God's goodness contrasted with the spirituality of her peers. In some ways, the inflexibility of Jansenism reflects the state of a childish soul. Fr. Groeschel writes that children typically attempt "to control or manipulate the Divine Being by prayer, supplication, and good works" (SP 67).

Similarly, psychologist Lawrence Kohlberg analyzed the way people respond to moral dilemmas. He proposed six stages of moral reasoning. His second stage is the stage of exchanging favors. Most elementary school students function at this level. They make moral decisions based on what will profit them. They are kind to others so that others will be kind to them.

Children can go beyond that to believe that if they are kind to one another without looking for repayment on earth, they will be rewarded in heaven. They tend to see each individual act as something for which they will receive a reciprocal reward.

I can inspire my boys—all pre-adolescents—by telling them they will get "prizes" in heaven for acts of charity. And this is the truth, but a simplistic, childish version of the truth. I hope that as they grow older they will do charitable acts out of true charity, rather than for the hope of a reward.

One day in the year before Zelie's death, Marie came home from boarding school with a string of beads to use to keep track of her virtuous acts. When Zelie saw them, she gave one to Celine. Then Therese wanted one as well. Little Therese and Celine carried their sacrifice beads around the house and garden, moving a bead along the string every time they overlooked each others' faults or went out of their way to be kind or obedient. Each bead was a gift to God.

For centuries, Catholics following the teaching of St. Ignatius of Loyola used beads to help with their Daily Examen. They moved a bead every time they failed to do God's will. Then at the end of the day they reviewed what each bead stood for, repented, confessed the sin silently, and resolved to do better tomorrow with God's grace.

The French Catholics of the nineteenth century turned this practice inside out. They began using beads to keep track of their merits, instead of their sins. Not only children did this. Adults too kept close track of the "points" they were making with God (HF 55). They overemphasized their good works.

Such practices have their place. They can inspire children and beginners. But they present a danger for many adults. They can distract us from the true purpose of our spiritual lives. The aim of our lives is to know, love, and serve God (CCC 1). God, not our works, is at the center of everything. Our relationship with him is a relationship of love.

God does not need our sacrifices, any more than he needed the sacrifices of bulls and goats in the Old Testament. In ancient times, Moses instructed the people to offer sacrifices to God as a sign of their repentance, gratitude, and conversion. Over the centuries, the Israelites made much of their sacrifices and ceremonies, but they stopped seeking God in their hearts. Their sacrifices became empty rituals.

The Israelites thought God would spare and even bless them because they followed the outward precepts of the law. They thought their sacrifices made them immune to his wrath. God sent prophets to warn them how wrong they were. When the people refused to listen to them, their enemies conquered them and sent them into exile. Ten tribes of Israel were completely lost to history in this way.

We can slip into a similar attitude, if we're not careful. Jesus told his disciples, "When you have done all that is commanded you, say, 'We are unworthy servants; we have only done what was our duty'" (Lk 10:17). God does not owe us anything, no matter how good we are. Rather, we owe something—indeed, everything—to God.

Expecting payment from God betrays a shallow understanding of the spiritual life. Yes, God will reward our good deeds and punish our sins. But we cannot earn heaven, no matter how many good things we have done. We cannot earn God's love.

If we are looking for reciprocity, we can find it in offering ourselves, rather than our good deeds, to God. When we give ourselves fully to him, he gives himself fully to us. That exchange is far from even. We receive more than we could ever give.

Therese never performed great deeds. As an adult, when she looked at her merits, she believed she had none to offer God. She did nothing extraordinary. Although she habitually avoided even venial sins, she knew that it was God's grace that kept her faithful. All she did was respond to it. God had made a smooth road for her to walk down, free from temptations towards mortal sin. What merit was there in the fact that she rarely stumbled? All her virtues were unmerited gifts.

By rejecting the notion that she had to do countless good works to earn God's friendship, Therese became free to trust in God's goodness, rather than her own. His faithfulness did not depend on hers. She could trust him as her all-loving Father. Would Louis withhold his love from his girls unless they did great things for him? Of course not! Then neither would God.

She did not have to work wonders in order to please God. She simply had to love him. Her confidence in him was childlike. She left more childish attitudes behind.

Forgetting our good works

St. Paul demonstrates his confidence in God in this way:

> If any other man thinks he has reason for confidence in the flesh, I have more: circumcised on the eighth day, of the people of Israel, of the tribe of Benjamin, a Hebrew born of Hebrews; as to the law a Pharisee, as to zeal a

> persecutor of the church, as to righteousness under the law blameless. But whatever gain I had, I counted as loss for the sake of Christ. Indeed I count everything as loss because of the surpassing worth of knowing Christ Jesus my Lord. For his sake I have suffered the loss of all things, and count them as refuse, in order that I may gain Christ and be found in him, not having a righteousness of my own, based on law, but that which is through faith in Christ. (Phil 3:4–9)

Elsewhere in his letters Paul calls himself the worst of sinners for having persecuted the Church before his conversion. But here he does not say he must let go of his past because it was so sinful. Instead, he says he must let go of everything that spoke in his favor. He must not rely on having been a strict practitioner of the Jewish faith, a natural heir of the Old Covenant. Instead of gaining him anything, these facts were no more than refuse—garbage. Who longs for garbage after he has thrown it away? Who brags about it or places confidence in it?

Paul continues:

> Not that I have already obtained this or am already perfect; but I press on to make it my own, because Christ Jesus has made me his own. Brethren, I do not consider that I have made it my own; but one thing I do, forgetting what lies behind and straining forward to what lies ahead, I press on toward the goal for the prize of the upward call of God in Christ Jesus. Let those of us who are mature be thus minded. (Phil 3:12–15)

Paul's goal is to die to himself and to the world. He is still on his journey. He is still striving for perfection. His confidence is in Christ, not his own strength. Since he belongs to Christ, he trusts that Christ will make him Christ-like. Paul calls such trust spiritual maturity.

This is the same perspective Therese had. Although she had received many graces from God, her confidence was not in any one grace, and certainly not in herself. Her confidence was in God alone. If God wanted her to be a saint, he would accomplish it.

How should we view optional devotions?

Remember the story Jesus told about the Pharisee and the tax collector?

> Two men went up to the temple to pray, one a Pharisee and the other a tax collector. The Pharisee, standing by himself, was praying thus, "God, I thank you that I am not like other people: thieves, rogues, adulterers, or even like this tax collector. I fast twice a week; I give a tenth of all my income . . ." (Lk 18:10–12)

St. Paul was a Pharisee before his conversion. The Pharisees adhered strictly to the Law of Moses. They created their own traditions that they believed helped them follow the Law more perfectly. The word *Pharisee* means one who is set apart. The Old Testament often calls holy objects *set apart* or consecrated for God's special use. Although we should certainly be set apart to do God's will, there is a connotation that the Pharisees were set apart *from other Jews*, implying that those who chose not to follow the Pharisees' traditions were not truly following God. Their goal was laudable, but in practice many of them became self-righteous.

This phenomenon is not particular to Biblical times. Even today we may be tempted to insist that there is only one right way of serving God. We might take optional devotions, spiritualities, or traditions and judge others by whether they follow them. Some might insist all devout women need to cover their heads at Mass. Others might believe that charismatic experiences are the signs of true openness to Christ. Still others might urge everyone to consecrate their lives to Mary, according to the teaching of St. Louis de Montfort.

All of these devotions or experiences are good in themselves. In fact most people in our day would benefit from more devotional practices, rather than less. Still we must vigilantly guard against demanding that everyone follow God in our particular way. Jesus upheld and fulfilled the Law of Moses, but did not follow the traditions of the Pharisees. The saints each practiced different devotions. Each of them was unique.

The Church requires plenty of practices of the faithful without our imposing more on our neighbors. The *Catechism* teaches us the essentials for prayer and the spiritual life. As childlike Christians, we must let God be God and let the Church be the Church. Our proper role is one of listening and obedience, not formulating doctrine. By all means, let us share with others the practices that have helped us grow closer to Christ. But if the Church does not call them essential, we must place no confidence in them. We must not judge others by whether they practice them. If these devotions hinder us from being humble and placing our confidence solely in God, they have become no more than refuse in our lives.

Pride goes before trust arrives

As I reflect on my life, I notice that pride long obstructed the way to trust. God gave me many blessings from the beginning. Our family, though not perfect, was stable. My parents' involvement in the Charismatic Renewal brought zeal and joy for serving God into the house. We prayed each morning as a family, went to daily Mass during Advent and Lent, and read and memorized whole chapters of the Bible. We attended weekly prayer meetings and Christian summer camp. My parents showed us the beauty of being open to life.

From a young age, I desired to be a saint. Friends and I built makeshift shrines on the school playground. My writing, which had begun almost as soon as I could read, often centered on Christian themes.

But pride threatened to kill my relationship with God. Instead of being humble and grateful for these graces, I considered myself better than my peers. I thought I was singled out for greatness and felt justified in judging and correcting others. Needless to say, this hurt my relationships with other people, which were already hard for me to develop since I was so painfully shy.

I was blind to my pride until I was about seventeen. It was another few years before I began battling it in earnest. Then, year after year, I cried out to God to help me become humble, while doing my best to fight my pride. But I was getting nowhere. I made no measurable progress.

Nothing, I believe, helps a person grow up like becoming a parent. Before marrying and having children, I thought I had all the answers about parenting (and almost everything else). Then I got married, conceived my first child, and was instantly nervous and unsure of myself. I decided to consult parenting experts.

I spent my pregnancy reading the works of child-rearing guru Dr. William Sears and Greg and Lisa Popcak. They were all proponents of the new ideal of attachment parenting. I became a (theoretical) expert on the subject. Once again, I thought I knew how parenting was supposed to look. I wrote up my plan for a natural childbirth. I hired a professional labor assistant.

Then real life hit me. When I was two weeks overdue with no contractions or dilation, my doctor convinced me to be induced. I checked into the hospital on Sunday morning with Dan at my side.

Like my mother, I have always had difficult veins for blood draws and IVs. Nurses poked me multiple times on both arms before they could take any blood. Then a lab assistant inserted an IV in the last free spot I had, my left wrist. It contained Pitocin, a synthetic hormone used to start contractions. The Pitocin didn't "take" that day or the next. At last on Tuesday, I called my labor assistant, Jessie, who had already gone home after one false start. My contractions had finally progressed from mild to moderate.

Jessie turned out to be a lapsed Catholic. Although we were paying her to help me through my contractions, she and Dan began discussing theology, temporarily forgetting about me. I had to keep reminding them that there is a time for everything!

My labor progressed slowly. By 4 P.M. on that third day, I was only dilated to three centimeters. My doctor broke my water to speed things up. Jessie pushed the stand my IV was connected to as she helped me walk up and down the hall. But the needle was not well secured. Just when my contractions were finally intensifying, the IV fell out. As soon as the Pitocin was no longer pumping into my body, my contractions stopped completely. I was virtually back at the beginning.

Now I had to make a decision. My doctor determined it was too late to restart induction that day. "We can try again tomorrow," she said. "But that's it. If it doesn't work, you'll need a C-section. Or you could have a C-section later tonight." Then she left, giving us half an hour to talk it over and decide.

The emotional ups and downs of those three days had almost overwhelmed me, although I had done a good job of suppressing my feelings. I began each morning with the thought I would be holding my baby in my arms by the end of the day, and here I was, hardly any closer to that reality. As it seemed unlikely that another day of induction would help, I tearfully agreed to a Caesarian birth.

Jessie and my doctor both thought I made the right choice. "You've been so patient," Jessie said. "You're gonna make a great mom." Little did she know that it was all a façade.

Our son was born at 11:03 P.M. We named him Dante after his grandfather.

I felt guilty and sad that I was not able to experience natural childbirth. But I was glad that my troubles were now over—or so I thought. In reality, they were just beginning.

For the first year of our marriage, I worked while Dan wrote his doctoral dissertation. Then I took twelve weeks off work, starting a week before my due date, because I did not want to go into labor on the job. With Dante's birth coming so much later than I had hoped, I was scheduled to go back to work when he was only nine weeks old. But I was not planning on going back. I thought that surely Dan would be working full time before then.

However, Dan was focused on finishing his dissertation. He had worked for years and spent thousands of dollars towards his philosophy degree. He wanted to finish it before we got married, but I was reluctant to wait any longer. We hoped to have more than a couple of children. Having no idea how easy it would be for us to conceive, or how long my fertility would last, I did not want to waste precious time.

With his education and resume, Dan thought finding a job would be easy. He planned to continue writing diligently until my leave was almost over. Then he would look for a non-demanding job that would leave his evenings free to continue his studies. I might have to go back to work for just a couple of weeks while he was looking. He thought that was a reasonable sacrifice to ask of me.

Unfortunately, we had not talked this over thoroughly. If we had, I would have been more mentally prepared and might not have reacted so negatively. I'm not sure. As it was, I had never considered the possibility of being a working mom, especially with an infant. The thought of spending even the working hours of two weeks away from Dante was anguishing. It was against all the parenting advice I had embraced. Now, instead of on-demand feedings, I would be nursing over my lunch hour and pumping during my breaks. Someone else (thankfully Dan, his mother, and mine) would be raising Dante, while I sat at a desk miles away.

But I also believed that when husband and wife disagreed, it was the man as the head of the household who should have the final word. I thought Dan's decision was misguided, but I followed it. I returned to work.

My first day back in the office, I caught a stomach virus from a co-worker. Besides having terrible chills, I was unable to keep anything down for three days. Dante was not getting enough nourishment through nursing and was screaming with hunger. Dan ran to the store and bought the dreaded infant formula.

Although my stomach was soon settled again and I returned to work after six extra days out, I ran a fever for two weeks straight. Even the doctor was concerned. I was still nursing Dante at night, until Dan put his foot down. I needed to take care of myself and get well. I never had gotten back to the point where I could supply all of Dante's nutrition. From now on, Dan would feed him formula at night, while I slept. I needed to do this to recover, but it was another psychological blow. No more co-sleeping. Even less time with my baby.

Dan was surprised to get no offers on jobs he had applied for. As my two weeks back at work turned into several, I struggled against guilt and resentment. I felt like we were putting Dante's future in jeopardy.

In an effort to find peace, I read *Abandonment to Divine Providence* by Fr. Jean-Pierre de Caussade. And one day I meditated on the verse, "My yoke is easy and my burden is light" (Mt 11:30).

"Easy?" I asked God in disbelief. "Light?" Was he kidding?

"*My* yoke," I felt God was saying back to me. "*My* burden."

Then I realized I had created my own yoke and burden with my preconceived ideas about parenthood. I was failing against a measure I created myself, not one that was written in stone. I had to admit that my ideal was not part of God's plan for me. This was difficult because I was so sure I was right! I really believed that following the attachment parenting dictates was the best thing I could do for Dante. But I had to set that belief aside. I needed to accept God's plan for my life. I needed to trust that he was in control, that circumstances had not gotten the better of him. He had not abandoned me and never would.

I took a deep breath and prayed, "Your will be done."

It's amazing how much easier life seemed after that. Going to work every day was still a yoke to bear. It was still a burden. But I could carry it now without resentment, because Jesus carried it with me. He had lifted its weight off my shoulders.

It was seven months before Dan called me at work to say he had been offered a job under Bishop Raymond L. Burke in La Crosse, Wisconsin. I was more than ready to move, if that's what it would take to be able to stay home. I put in my notice the first chance I could.

Some attachment-parenting-hard-liners might criticize our actions. They might say that we failed to be the parents we should have been. They might even suspect that the eventual peace I found was not from God at all, but just a psychological masking of my guilt. Thankfully, we are not accountable to them. We are accountable to God. He alone will judge whether we did the best we could at that time and place.

I did not fail at my vocation as wife and mother. Our marriage was not adversely affected, as it could have been had I not taken a first step towards trusting God. I thank God for the grace that he gave us. And I trust that Dante received all the love and attention he needed.

What if . . . ?

Sometimes when life is not going the way we wish, we are tempted to ask what would have happened if our circumstances were different. I have sometimes wondered what my life would have been like if my sister Terri had lived. I was never close to my two other sisters during childhood, because our ages were so far apart. Terri was four years older than me, and already at age six I had a special love for her. Her temperament was similar to mine. I believe we would have been close had she survived.

I had lots of friends in my early years. But after our move of 1,500 miles to Minneapolis, soon followed by another school change, I found it harder to make new friends. I seldom opened up to anyone any longer. My tendency to suppress my feelings became more entrenched. I did not trust other people to understand me or be sympathetic towards me.

My late childhood could have been completely different had Terri survived.

But asking, *what if?* is another trap. The Devil particularly likes to tempt us with it. It's easy to dream up scenarios in which life would be more comfortable, and we would be happier or holier. But they are fantasies. God sets each one of us in the place and time that he desires. He does not actively will everything bad that happens in our lives. He does use them, however. We can only live the life we have.

In some cases God asks us to change our circumstances. In all cases he asks us to let him *change us* by grace. We can only change so much of our exterior world. Our interior world is where God dwells and acts in a particular way.

What if? or, *if only,* can make us dissatisfied with our lives to the point that we miss the grace God is offering us here and now. Such thinking can foster pride. *Well, if God gave me the same grace he gave Therese, I would be a saint too,* we might think. It can erode our trust. God knows what he is doing in our lives. Our circumstances have not gotten the better of him.

The only *what if?* we should consider asking is, *What if I were to give myself totally to God?* But better than asking it would be choosing to do it.

Therese's Christmas conversion

The Martin family always attended Midnight Mass on Christmas Eve. The children each placed a pair of shoes in the corner by the fireplace, and Louis filled them with presents after Mass.

This French Christmas custom is still enjoyed today. Many children have special wooden clogs modeled on peasants' shoes just for the Christmas celebration. Some children receive their gifts from Père Noël (Father Christmas). The Martin girls were always visited by the Child Jesus. In former years, Celine and Therese had gathered shoes and boots from all over the house to set out for him. Their childish enthusiasm was rewarded with dolls, bags of candy, and clog-shaped sugar cakes (see LT 1219). The girls opened their gifts on Christmas morning when they were little, but in later years examined their shoes after Mass.

Celine no longer put her shoes out. She was practically grown up. But she resisted Therese's natural growth towards maturity. After all, Therese was the youngest. When she grew up, their childhood traditions would be over. Wanting to keep up the ritual that everyone loved, she encouraged Therese to continue putting her Christmas shoes out every year. Louis also enjoyed the pleasure it gave his daughters.

Now Therese was nearly fourteen, however, long past the age to believe in "magic shoes" (SS 98). Arriving home after Mass, Louis spied Therese's shoes and sighed. He was weary and would have liked to go to bed. Therese was running up the stairs to put her hat away, her heart filled with the joy of having received the Eucharist, and anticipation of the surprises ahead. Celine followed behind her. "Well," Louis said to himself, but loud enough that both the girls heard him, "fortunately, this will be the last year" (ibid.).

Instantly, tears stung Therese's eyes. She slowed her ascent and turned her head to look at Celine, who had approached her with concern. They had almost reached the landing above. Celine's face displayed a sympathetic sadness. She knew how easily her sister was moved to tears. "Oh, Therese, don't go downstairs," she said. "It would cause you too much grief to look at your slippers right now!" (ibid.).

But suddenly, Therese's oversensitivity was gone. She forced herself not to cry and ran back down the stairs with a pounding heart. As though she had heard nothing, she picked up her shoes and joyfully exclaimed over each item her father had filled them with. She laughed sincerely. Soon Louis was laughing too, while Celine looked on with gaping mouth. Was this the same Therese?

The saint would later call this change miraculous. Just as the Virgin had cured her instantly from her illness when she was ten, God had transformed her in an instant from a sensitive little girl into a mature young woman. He healed the deep wounds from losing her mother, and her emotional fragility with them. Never again would her feelings overwhelm her. Never again would her family have to be careful what they said in her presence.

Yet there was a significant difference in the two events. This time, Therese experienced no outward signs of God's intervention. In accordance with her ordinary way of holiness, God changed her heart quietly. The proof came with her ability to overcome herself.

Therese had not stood around idly waiting for God to act. She had fought valiantly against her inclinations. But in this area of her emotions, she made no headway until God stepped in. She writes, "Jesus, satisfied with my goodwill, accomplished in an instant what I had been unable to do in ten years" (SS 98). Hard work had not changed her, but only God's grace. Nevertheless, her work was not finished. She still struggled against her feelings, but now she triumphed over them. God gave her the grace to overcome temptation, but she remained free to choose whether to co-operate with it. Time and again she did so, restraining anger, sadness, and annoyance out of love for Christ.

Now that Therese had finally passed this milestone, she might have thought her way would be smooth and easy for a time. But a new challenge to her trust was just around the next curve.

Questions for Reflection

1. How has God blessed me throughout the years? Am I grateful?

2. Do I place too much confidence in my abilities? Have I searched for security in God's gifts, rather than in God himself?

3. How do God's plans for my life right now appear different from mine? Can I sincerely say, "Your will be done?"

4. Have I put more burdens on myself than God wills through my unrealistic expectations for life? How can I take up God's yoke instead?

Practical Suggestions

* Read Part 3 of the *Catechism* on Life in Christ. Resolve to read part of it daily for Advent, Lent, or the calendar year. Learn what the Church deems essential to the spiritual life.

* Examine the devotions and practices that you hold dear. Are any distracting you from God or barring the way to humility? Prayerfully consider if you should give any of them up in order to grow in trust, or if you can change your attitude while retaining them. This calls for discernment. Many devotions that are not essential for everyone are nonetheless helpful to some. Do not be scrupulous here. If you choose to retain them, return to this reflection often, to make sure you have not given in to pride.

Chapter Six
Waiting and Working

Be still before the LORD, *and wait patiently for him.*

Ps 37:7

Soon after she learned Pauline was to enter the Carmelite monastery, Therese became convinced that she also was called to be a Carmelite nun. She was not, as we might suspect, just seeking to be reunited with her beloved sister. She insists that from the beginning she longed to be closer to Jesus (SL 58).

Therese's "Christmas conversion" intensified the call. In the following months, she felt a growing urge to enter the order by Christmas Eve. What a way to mark the anniversary of her conversion!

But there was one major obstacle: her age. In 1887, she was only fourteen, much younger than anyone who had ever entered the Lisieux Carmel before. At first Therese did not appear to recognize this obstacle.

She was more concerned with her father's reaction. Marie and Pauline were already living behind the cloister grille. Leonie returned home after a failed attempt to join the Poor Clares. She later asked Louis' permission to join the Visitation sisters. Louis consented, although Leonie was still living at home for the time being. Only Celine and Therese would remain with their father when Leonie left.

Then on May 1 Louis suffered a stroke. His left side was temporarily paralyzed. Thanks to the quick-thinking Uncle Isidore, Louis recovered the use of his limbs. But he remained frailer than before. Could he endure the shock of losing his little Queen?

Therese knew she had to speak. She had delayed long enough. She always saw dates as important in her spiritual life. She decided Pentecost was the perfect time to speak to him.

All day she was anxious as she looked for an opportunity to see him alone. What if she lost her courage? "Holy Apostles," she prayed, "by entering Carmel, I wish to be an apostle to the apostles on earth today. I seek to pray and sacrifice for God's holy priests. I know you will not refuse to listen to my prayer. Please ask our divine Savior to give me strength. Teach me what to say to Papa."

Her opportunity finally came after the family prayed Evening Prayer. Louis went out into the garden by himself. Therese found him, hands folded on his lap, sitting by the well and listening to the "evening song" of the birds (SS 107). He looked like he was silently praising the God of creation.

Therese could not stop her tears as she sat down beside him. He tenderly laid her head on his heart. "What's the matter, my little Queen?" he asked (ibid.).

As Therese tried to gather her courage, Louis rose slowly, keeping her head on his chest. She had grown physically as well as spiritually. Tall and stately, she fit neatly under his arm.

Therese took a deep breath. "Papa, I want to enter Carmel as soon as possible," she said. "God is calling me, and I do not want to put him off." She felt a tear fall from his eye and mingle with those that were already running down her cheeks.

"Are you certain, Therese?" he asked without looking down at her. "You are very young. Could not the good God wait for you a while? Perhaps you will change your mind in time."

"Oh, no, Papa. I will never change my mind. I long to give everything to God and to pray for his priests. Where else could I do this as well as in Carmel?"

Louis listened in silence as she told him how the desire to enter Carmel had grown within her, and how she had increasingly felt called to save souls since Christmas.

Then he led her to the wall of the garden, where some drooping saxifrage plants were blooming. Their reddish buds opened here and there to become fragile white flowers. Picking one, he mused, "You see this little flower? God himself created it, cared for it, and made it grow. But now he is plucking it from its native soil to plant it in other ground." He handed the flower to Therese, roots and all.

She beamed up at him. Papa understood! His face, no longer troubled, was flooded with joy.

Therese placed the flower in her copy of *The Imitation of Christ*, her favorite guide to the spiritual life. She would keep it there for years as a reminder of her father's loving sacrifice and God's providence in her life.

Now she had to approach Uncle Isidore. Therese also needed his permission before she could choose her vocation in life. Uncle Isidore had never understood Therese's character. He was gentle with her, but denied her request. He forbade her to bring up the subject again until she was seventeen at least. Perhaps he hoped that by then she would think better of the idea. "The Carmelite Order is not for children, Therese," he said. "It is for mature Christians on their way to sanctity. I respect the order too much to press for a child to enter it. And what would our neighbors and friends say? They would think we had lost all sense. No, it would take a miracle for me to rethink this. You must wait."

Wait? Therese returned home sad. Eleven days later, darkness engulfed her. Jesus, to whom she had been so close, hid from her sight. For three days, she suffered the desolation of being abandoned. At last, no longer able to endure it, she took the audacious step of approaching her uncle again on the fourth day. When she asked to speak with him, he invited her into his study.

"I prayed about our conversation," he began before she could address him. "I did not ask God to perform a miracle. Instead, I asked him for a simple change of my heart, if it was truly his will for you to enter Carmel so young. He answered my prayer. You are a little flower that God wishes to gather to himself. I will not oppose your entrance."

Immediately, light filled Therese's soul. She believed God *had* performed a miracle. Who but God could have changed Uncle Isidore's mind in such a short time? His use of the flower metaphor further confirmed that God was at work.

But Therese's waiting was far from over. Joyfully she went the next day to tell Sr. Agnes (Pauline) that she was free to enter Carmel. Another blow awaited. Fr. Delatroette, the superior of the Lisieux Carmel, had already spoken with the nuns about the matter. He said he could not let Therese enter before she was twenty-one.

Wait more than six years? Impossible!

Therese and Louis went themselves to see Fr. Delatroette. He refused to budge, only saying that if the bishop of Bayeux, whose delegate he was, agreed to let Therese enter, then he would consent as well.

Therese returned home in tears, vowing that if the bishop refused his consent, she would take her plea to the pope! And that is what occurred. Bishop Hugonin would not make a decision without meeting with Fr. Delatroette. Therese had already decided to join a local pilgrimage to Rome, accompanied by her father and Celine. That pilgrimage would begin in only three days. The bishop promised to send the Martins a letter in Italy with the outcome of his meeting.

Waiting with hope

What happens when we know God's will for our lives, yet we do not see it being fulfilled? This chapter explores the tension between hope and unfulfilled desire. We'll consider how Abraham acted, when God's promise of a son remained unaccomplished. We'll see what the *Catechism* says about the two types of presumption. I'll share how God made me wait to find a husband. We'll discuss the dangers of superstitions. Finally, we'll learn what made Fr. Delatroette change his mind about Therese.

The Bible says, "Hope deferred makes the heart sick, but a desire fulfilled is a tree of life" (Prv 13:12). Therese experienced this sickness of heart with her uncle's initial opposition to her entrance to Carmel. After he changed his mind, she did not fall back into darkness as great when others opposed her. It still grieved her, however. "My heart was plunged into bitterness, but into peace too, for I was seeking God's will," she wrote (SS 109).

Often we struggle to discern God's will for our lives. Which job offer should we accept? Which school should we attend? How should we try to repair a broken relationship? God expects us to use our reason to find the way.

But other times, especially when our life's vocation is at stake, God makes his will clear to us in our hearts. He might plant an attraction to marriage, the priesthood, or religious life so firmly in our souls that we recognize his call. That does not mean we will easily or quickly reach our goal.

Therese did not just sit back and let God do all the work to open the doors of Carmel. She did everything she could to see her desire fulfilled. Beginning with her second approach to her uncle, her resolve overpowered her timidity.

At last—nearly a month after the visit to the bishop—the day came for the pilgrims' audience with Pope Leo XIII. No letter had come from

Bishop Hugonin. Therese would have to ask permission of the Holy Father.

Fr. Reverony, vicar general of Bayeux, led the pilgrimage. He knew about Therese's desire to enter Carmel early. He had received Louis and Therese when they visited Bishop Hugonin to seek his permission. Fr. Reverony forbade the pilgrims to speak when they came before the pope one by one. They must not prolong their audience! But bold Celine came to Therese's aid. "Speak!" she whispered in her sister's ear as Therese's turn to approach the papal throne arrived.

Pope Leo sat before them, the authority of his office in evidence. Therese knelt and kissed his slipper. He held out his hand for her to kiss his ring. Instead, she clasped her own hands and pleaded with tears, "Most Holy Father, I have a great favor to ask you! In honor of your Jubilee, permit me to enter Carmel at the age of fifteen!" (SL 134).

The pope did not understand. He turned to Fr. Reverony, who was standing nearby. Fr. Reverony quickly explained, emphasizing that Therese was *only a child!*

Pope Leo turned back to Therese. "You will enter if God wills it," he said (SL 135). And then the audience was over. Therese opened her mouth to address him again. Two Swiss guards approached and touched her arms, indicating she needed to move on. When she did not do so, they lifted her by the elbows, and with the help of Fr. Reverony, carried her to the door.

Now Therese's efforts to answer God's call were ended. All that remained were prayer and trust. Profoundly sad, she felt sure at the same time that somehow God would make the way to fulfill his will.

God's promise to Abraham

The Old Testament provides another story of trusting God's plan in the face of obstacles.

God spoke to Abraham, commanding him to leave the land of Ur where his family dwelled and to travel to an unknown land that God would give to him and his descendants. Abraham obeyed. He packed up everyone and set out, eventually reaching Canaan. Years passed. He was growing old, and was still just a sojourner. God spoke with him again and promised him a son. Through this son, his descendants would inherit the land (Gn 15).

Abraham believed God would fulfill his promise. However, his wife Sarah did not conceive. By the time he was ninety-nine, he no longer knew what God expected of him. How could God keep his word?

At last, Sarah offered Abraham her maidservant (slave) Hagar as a concubine. If Hagar bore a son, everyone would consider him to be Sarah's son, Abraham's heir. Abraham accepted the offer (Gn 16).

Some Bible commentators, mainly non-Catholics, say that Abraham committed serious sin in taking Hagar as his concubine. Certainly Christianity teaches monogamy. But if we look at Abraham in the context of his time, we find extenuating circumstances. First, the arrangement Sarah proposed was a common one in the ancient Near East. The Code of Hammurabi includes rules governing such arrangements *(A New Catholic Commentary on Sacred Scripture*, Orchard, et. al. New York: Nelson, 1953, 193). Second, God had not communicated anything to Abraham about sexual mores. Unlike Adam and Eve, Abraham and Sarah did not disobey a command God had given them.

Abraham, like Therese, tried to do his part to bring about God's will in his life. At first he had waited for Sarah to have a son naturally, but that had not happened. So he was willing to try another arrangement. He made the wrong choice. In taking Hagar as his concubine, he thought he was furthering God's plan. His actions actually hindered it. Hagar and her son Ishmael caused strife within the family.

Later, God appeared to Abraham and promised that *Sarah* would have a son (Gn 17). God made it clear that Sarah's son was the child he had earlier promised Abraham. Abraham laughed. Still, he believed God, even though God's way of fulfilling the promise seemed impossible.

At that point, Abraham could do nothing more to bring about God's plan, besides having normal relations with his wife. He had to let go and simply trust.

Working with God

Two extremes lead us off the road of trust. One says that if God has promised us something, we can sit back and do nothing. He will accomplish it on his own. This seems pious and trusting, but it may conceal laziness. It may also indicate mistrust. Perhaps we think that if God doesn't fulfill his promise, at least we have lost nothing. After all, we expended no effort. And if we keep quiet about God's promises, no one can ridicule us when nothing happens.

Inaction may also betray presumption. For example, some Christians believe that God promises his true followers an eternity in heaven no matter what they do. So instead of trying to obey God's commands, they expect God to overlook even their unrepentant sin. What a dangerous way to live! What a false trust!

> There are two kinds of *presumption*. Either man presumes upon his own capacities, (hoping to be able to save himself without help from on high), or he presumes upon God's almighty power or his mercy (hoping to obtain his forgiveness without conversion and glory without merit). (CCC 2092)

At the other extreme, then, lies another kind of presumption. We cannot expect to fulfill all God's plans through our work. We have to know when to let go. Therese did everything reasonable and moral to accomplish God's will. When she ran out of options, she suffered, but did not despair. God was teaching her to rely on his power, rather than her own.

In the same way, we cannot earn our salvation through our efforts. St. Paul strikes the balance between the two types of presumption when he teaches,

> Therefore, my beloved, just as you have always obeyed me, not only in my presence, but much more now in my absence, work out your own salvation with fear and trembling; for it is God who is at work in you, enabling you both to will and to work for his good pleasure. (Phil 2:12–13)

God and man must work together. Our efforts do not suffice, but God has made us his partner, his bride. God gives us the great gift of true participation in accomplishing his plan. It dignifies our humanity.

Think of a toddler who wants to help his mother with the chores. She knows he is too little to do much. He will be slow and clumsy. She will need to direct him through every step. At this age, he hinders more than helps her. But she sees his desire to be like her. She lets him help for his benefit, rather than hers. How good he feels when he has finished the job and she praises him!

We are like that child in relationship to God. God allows us to work alongside him and thus become more like him. He does this for our good.

We can never, of course, do evil for the good end of seeing God's will come to pass. If God had previously forbidden Abraham to take a concubine and he had done it anyway, God may have chosen someone else with whom to establish his covenant. Or else he would have required

Abraham to repent. That repentance would surely have been recorded in the Bible as a lesson for the rest of us. Doing evil to obtain a good result is antithetical to the Gospel (see Romans 3:8).

Sometimes the accomplishment of God's will requires a miracle. Then, like Abraham, we must learn to wait patiently.

Waiting for Mr.—er . . .

Remember the saying *Waiting for Mr. Right?* Although my maiden name was Wright, my single years did seem to be more about waiting than working.

I sat on the sidelines through high school and college, while classmates dated and got engaged. Looking back I see that some of the young men I was infatuated with were not at all suitable. My shyness probably saved me from making terrible mistakes. But it was painful at the time.

After college graduation, I spent two years as a lay missionary just outside of Tokyo, Japan. I taught English Conversation, supporting the evangelization efforts of Fr. James Hyatt, an American priest.

One day when a Japanese friend and I were site-seeing together, she gave me an *omamori*, a Japanese good-luck charm. A small piece of embroidered silk purchased at a Shinto shrine, it enclosed a piece of paper with a request. This one was meant to bring a happy marriage. Thinking I could use all the help I could get, I slipped it into my purse. I carried the omamori around with me for a few weeks, at first thinking nothing of it, then feeling guiltier and guiltier about it. At last I admitted to myself that a good-luck charm had no place in the life of a Catholic missionary. I threw it out without telling my friend, and confessed my sin.

I have since learned that omamori are petitions to the deities enshrined at the purchase site. So I was unknowingly praying to false gods to help me find a husband.

Another, more harmless, Japanese tradition centered on Girls' Day.

On March 3, Japanese girls display their *hina* dolls, representations of the emperor and empress, and sometimes the entire court. Tradition says that setting out your hina dolls will ensure you get married, while leaving them out too long after the festival ends will mean a late marriage.

Students gave me miniscule hina dolls that I still possess. I still put them out when I remember to do so. I love Asian culture and artistry. I never considered the hina dolls as good-luck charms. To me they were simply a way of celebrating femininity and Japanese culture. But even seemingly harmless traditions can subtly affect our thinking.

A few years after returning to the United States, I was talking to a friend of mine who was recently engaged. Naturally, the subject of marriage came up. "I've always felt called to marriage," I said. "But lately I have this feeling that I'm going to remain single."

"Really?" My friend was incredulous. "Why?"

I couldn't say at the time, but later I realized it was because I had forgotten to put out my hina dolls that year! I laughed at myself.

For over four years beginning in my late twenties, I shared an apartment with a friend who had grown up in the same charismatic community I had. Sarah committed to be a member as an adult also. I was drawn in another direction. During those years I joined the Carmelites. However, we both worked for a time with the Fellowship of the Holy Spirit, an outreach to introduce people to the charismatic gifts and a deeper relationship with Christ.

While we were roommates, Sarah dated one man for several months. After they broke up, another man that she had been interested in years ago came back into her life. They eventually married.

I found the wedding and reception unexpectedly difficult. I actually cried in public during the dance—an almost unheard of thing for me. Fortunately, the dim light in the reception hall obscured my tears. I don't think anyone noticed. At thirty-one years old I had absolutely no marriage prospects. I did not know a single man I would have been interested in dating, even if any had asked me out.

I returned to the apartment alone. For the next couple of weeks, I packed up my possessions and scrubbed the apartment clean. (Sarah returned to help me with this latter task.) Then I moved to a one-bedroom apartment.

Friends, acquaintances, and co-workers began feeling sorry for me. Some set me up with their single male friends and family members. By this point, I was trying to be open. I realized I would probably have to give up some of the things I desired in a husband. So I went on a blind date with a Lutheran, with a man who had just started to get serious about his Catholic faith, and with a couple of others whose interests and hobbies differed greatly from mine. Nothing came of any of them.

Then one spring day I was reading *The National Catholic Register* and saw a front-page interview with Barbara Nicolosi. She had started a school to train Catholics to be screenwriters. Act One was planning a special one-month intensive program for August. I decided to look into it further. Maybe my life needed a new direction. I could sublet my apartment for a month and see if I could start a new career.

I never made the move. The next issue of the *Register* contained an interview with Anthony Buono. Anthony ran a website called Single Catholics Online (SCOL). A year's membership was $60. Online dating services were in their infancy. I had never heard of a Catholic one until then.

I thought over joining for the next few days. I knew that if I signed up, I would have to keep it secret from my family, at least at first. I wanted neither teasing nor over-the-top enthusiasm. I just wanted to look quietly for a potential spouse. I checked out the website and liked what I saw. Each member created a profile by responding to specific questions such as: What is your favorite devotion? Do you prefer Mass in Latin or

English? What is your favorite hymn? What one word would you use to describe your character?

I felt sheepish, but I signed up.

I spent an entire evening writing and re-writing answers to the profile questions. Favorite devotion: the Divine Mercy Chaplet. Language of Liturgy: English. Favorite hymn: Let All Mortal Flesh Keep Silence. Character: loyal.

Then my profile went live.

I decided to do nothing more for two weeks. Then, if no Catholic men had contacted me through my SCOL inbox, I would contact some of them. While I waited, I browsed through the profiles of men in my age range. I went through 200 of them, taking notes on the ones I found most interesting.

As I had feared, at the end of two weeks no one had contacted me. So I chose the two men whose profiles most intrigued me and sent both a message. One was a part-time actor in New York. The other was a philosophy student in Washington, D.C. named Dan.

Later Dan would tell me that he had just re-read my SCOL profile the night before I contacted him. He liked a lot of what he read. But he hesitated to contact me because I said I was shy. He had had a negative experience in the past with a shy date.

Dan and I rarely had trouble keeping a conversation going. Our first date, two months after we met online, lasted seven hours. Eleven months later we were married.

Since I turned eighteen, I had prayed regularly that God would develop in my future husband the qualities I needed and desired, and develop in me the qualities he needed and desired in a wife. After thinking I would have to compromise in order not to remain single my whole life, I rejoiced to find that my prayers had been answered. I discovered that Eagan, Minnesota was Dan's home base. His parents lived (and still do today) only ten minutes from mine.

God did not let me be passive in finding a husband. He required me to do more than I was comfortable with. I had to take the first step and contact Dan. God used me to answer my prayers.

Choosing prayer, not superstition

Good-luck charms seek to manipulate God, spirits, nature, or other people. A "lucky shirt" worn to a football game might seem harmless. Horoscopes and tarot cards are not.

> A sound Christian attitude consists in putting oneself confidently into the hands of Providence for whatever concerns the future, and giving up all unhealthy curiosity about it.
>
> All forms of divination are to be rejected. . . . Consulting horoscopes, astrology, palm reading, interpretation of omens and lots, the phenomena of clairvoyance, and recourse to mediums all conceal a desire for power over time, history, and, in the last analysis, other human beings, as well as a wish to conciliate hidden powers. They contradict the honor, respect, and loving fear that we owe to God alone.
>
> All practices of magic or sorcery . . . are gravely contrary to the virtue of religion. . . . Wearing charms is also reprehensible. (CCC 2115–17)

Sometimes we can even misuse prayer and other spiritual practices, turning them into a form of magic. Prayer is not a way to oblige God to do what we want. It is not even primarily about petitioning him. The *Catechism* lists four types of prayer besides petition: blessing and adoration, intercession, thanksgiving, and praise. Blessing and adoration take the first place. They acknowledge that God is our omnipotent and loving Creator. Prayer develops a deep relationship with God (see CCC 2623–42).

In the previous chapter, we discussed how good devotions can become harmful if we pride ourselves on them, or judge other people by whether they practice them. A third way we can misuse devotions is by treating them as magic.

Some people misuse the brown scapular in this way. Centuries ago the Virgin Mary promised salvation to Carmelites who wore the brown scapular that was part of their habit. It was understood that they must be faithful to the Carmelite Rule of Life. The devotion eventually spread to Catholics outside the Carmelite order. The small brown scapular was a sign of their commitment to Carmelite spirituality, and especially Carmelite devotion to Mary.

Unfortunately, some people have misused it as insurance against hell. A former co-worker of mine lived a life of gravely immoral behavior. I do not know that he ever went to Church. But he proudly wore the brown scapular under his shirt.

Now, I cannot judge what went on in his soul. Perhaps devotion to Mary lingered in his heart from his childhood. Perhaps he wore the scapular as a plea for help—"Do not forget me, even though I am unworthy!" But he *appeared* to use it as a good-luck charm, a hope for salvation without any attempt or desire to repent.

No object—not even Christ's Body and Blood in the Eucharist—can gain us salvation without our cooperation. Again, God has chosen to make us a real part of his plan for creation. We must participate, by opening our hearts to him.

Jesus said that we should get rid of everything that causes us to sin—even (metaphorically) our hands and eyes (see Mt 5:29–30). If I have trusted in devotions, the sacraments, or any other religious practices as though they were magic, I need to repent and reform my attitude.

Our trust must reside in God alone.

Fr. Delatroette changes his mind

Although Therese's trip to Rome did not end the way she had hoped, God was working out his plan. The Martins returned home to Lisieux, still hearing nothing from Bishop Hugonin about his meeting with Fr. Delatroette.

Sr. Agnes advised Therese to write to the bishop to remind him of his promise, in case he had forgotten. Therese mailed the letter just before Christmas. At midnight Mass she experienced great disappointment. She had planned on celebrating this Christmas in Carmel.

On New Year's Day, Mother Marie de Gonzague informed Therese that she had received a letter from the bishop on December 28, giving Therese permission to enter Carmel early. But now the prioress herself chose to delay. She would open the cloister door to Therese only after Lent.

To Therese, the three additional months of waiting appeared the worst of all. But at least she knew that at the end of them she would attain her desire.

We do not know what made Fr. Delatroette change his mind. Presumably, the bishop persuaded him. Lest we think he was too harsh in resisting Therese's request, Gorres surmises that the whole town would have known about Leonie's failed attempt at religious life. She returned home for a second time while Therese was waiting to enter Carmel, leaving the Visitation convent that January after only seven months. Should the superior of Carmel give her sister—the reputed coddled baby of the family—special permission to enter the Carmelites early? (HF 146).

Even after allowing Therese to enter, Fr. Delatroette remained unconvinced that she should be there. Louis' illness delayed her taking of the habit. Then Fr. Delatroette postponed her profession eight months. But eventually he saw her worth. Therese exercised impressive physical strength and good sense in caring for the other sisters when a devastating flu epidemic hit the convent. "She shows great promise for this community," he said (SL 120). This was in 1891. Therese had already been a Carmelite for more than four years. She worked faithfully to prove her vocation, and at last God crowned her efforts.

Questions for Reflection

1. Do I expect God to do all the work in my spiritual life? Do I try to do all the work myself? Or do I see the spiritual life as collaboration between myself and God?

2. Have I used magic, good-luck charms, or sacramentals and devotions as a means of manipulating God, others, or creation?

Practical Suggestions

* If you are waiting for God's will to be fulfilled, make a list of the steps you have taken to help bring it about. Now brainstorm what else you can do. Put at least one of these ideas on your calendar or to-do list.

* Examine the reasons God may be making you wait. Is he teaching you humility and trust? Are you physically, psychologically, spiritually, and in every other way ready for fulfillment of your desires? Pray about ways you can grow while waiting.

Chapter Seven
Anger, Annoyance, and Other Negative Emotions

Let every man be quick to hear, slow to speak, slow to anger, for the anger of man does not work the righteousness of God.

Jas 1:19–20

Therese had no delusions about the severity of Carmelite life when she entered the Carmel of Lisieux on April 9, 1888. She may not have been prepared for the trials that the other nuns brought her, however. Some sisters were far from being saints!

Catholic women in nineteenth century France had two options: marriage or religious life. Parents virtually arranged marriages for their daughters. Undoubtedly, some of the nuns did not have true religious vocations. Some later left. One particularly troublesome sister ended her life in a mental institution.

When Therese entered Carmel at age fifteen, Marie Martin, now Sr. Marie of the Sacred Heart was still a novice. Marie expected to continue her privileged place in Therese's life as her mentor and guide. After all, besides being Therese's most recent mother-figure, Marie was her godmother. Many of the nuns assumed the older Martin sisters would continue to baby Therese.

But Therese amazed them by insisting she remain independent to follow God's will. Marie opposed Therese's early entrance into Carmel. Without being at all bitter about this, Therese saw that Marie's will for her did not necessarily correspond with God's. She had grown up since Marie left home. If she was mature enough to be a Carmelite, she did not need babying. She stood on God's grace and direction. Therese came to Carmel for Jesus, not to be with her sisters. Carmel was not Les Buissonnets.

Similarly, during her novitiate Therese worked with Sr. Agnes in the refectory. The nuns normally kept silence outside of recreation and communal prayer times. But they had permission to speak, in as few words as possible, in order to do their duty. Mother Marie de Gonzague enforced this rule laxly. So Sr. Agnes tried to use her time with Therese to renew their old confidences. Therese gently rebuffed her. This sister too misunderstood the state of Therese's soul.

Other nuns presented further challenges. "Of course, one does not have enemies in Carmel," Therese later wrote, "but still there are natural attractions, one feels drawn to a certain sister, whereas you go a long way around to avoid meeting another" (SL 93). How can a person check these natural inclinations, being charitable towards everyone? Therese fought this battle daily.

As the prioress and later novice mistress during Therese's years in Carmel, Mother Marie de Gonzague was a special case. She had known Therese since Pauline's entrance. From the beginning she encouraged Therese in her vocation and called her "Teresita," after the young niece of St. Teresa of Avila. She worked for Therese's early entrance into Carmel. But then she delayed that entrance for three months after Fr. Delatroette granted his permission for it, perhaps as a compromise with him. The best adjective we can use for her may be *changeable*. Gorres calls her an "alternately radiant and dark personality" (HF 202).

Shortly after Therese's entrance, Mother Marie de Gonzague wrote a letter to Therese's aunt, Celine Guerin. She praised Therese as "perfect" (SL 91). For her part Therese liked the prioress so much that sometimes when passing her room she had to grasp the banister to keep from knocking on her door.

This relationship threatened to bar the way to trust. Therese needed to depend on God alone for her joy. The Carmelite Rule forbade the nuns to have "particular friendships," affection for fellow nuns that could cause favoritism and division. In this area too the prioress relaxed the Rule. Many of the nuns had affection for Mother Marie de Gonzague that went beyond the respect due to a superior. A Mother-Marie faction existed behind the convent walls. Therese refused to cling too tightly to any human being.

Later, a rivalry developed between Mother Marie de Gonzague and Sr. Agnes, after the latter was elected prioress. Therese considered them both her mothers in different ways. She rejoiced that she had never taken sides.

Providentially for Therese, life under Mother Marie de Gonzague was not always pleasant. The prioress tested her vocation. The novice mistress assigned Therese to weed the garden daily. Mother Marie, ignorant of the assignment, criticized Therese for always taking a walk during the afternoon. Therese did not correct her misunderstanding of the situation. Nor did she harbor resentment. The prioress also ordered Therese to kiss the floor as a sign of humility almost every time they met.

Mother Marie was only one of many difficult sisters in the monastery. An elderly lay sister, Sr. St. Vincent-de-Paul, called Therese "the grand lady." Perhaps Therese's height and stately walk won her that title, for she was certainly neither rich nor proud, nor apt to rule over others. St. Vincent ridiculed Therese's skill with embroidery and manual labor as well—ridicule that was most likely fair, but still hard to hear with humility. Therese responded by smiling at her. And when the sister remarked that Therese would never do anything useful for the convent, Therese silently and peacefully agreed (SL 93).

Unable to do menial tasks well, and unsuited for great spiritual deeds, Therese searched for opportunities to perform small acts of charity. Every evening one nun needed to assist elderly and infirm Sr. St. Pierre to walk from the chapel to the refectory for dinner. Therese volunteered for the task, even though she knew this sister was difficult to endure.

Ten minutes before the nuns finished praying mental prayer, St. Pierre shook her hour glass impatiently. It was time to go. Therese, who sat directly behind her, rose at once. Had she followed her feelings, she would not have moved at all. She knew complaints and criticisms awaited her. But she forced herself to act as if the nun were Jesus himself. She picked up the sister's bench, feeling disapproving eyes upon her clumsy movements.

Then St. Pierre began to walk, with Therese holding onto the cincture rope encircling the other nun's waist. St. Pierre stumbled slightly. "You're going too fast!" she burst out. "I'm going to break something." Therese obediently slowed down. "I can't feel your hand," came the next complaint. "You're not holding onto me. I'm going to fall. I knew you were too young when you asked to do this task!" (See SS 248–49.) Somehow they reached the refectory with limbs, if not nerves, intact.

Therese eased St. Pierre into a chair. She carefully turned back the nun's sleeves in the way she always demanded.

Then she was free to leave. Inwardly, she wished to retreat as quickly as possible. Hesitating a moment, however, she watched the gnarled, pain-filled hands of the old nun fumble trying to cut her bread, and drop her knife. Therese quietly retrieved the utensil and cut the bread for her. St. Pierre looked up in surprise. Therese beamed down upon her.

She performed this service for seven years (HF 243).

At another period in her life in Carmel, Therese experienced a different trial during mental prayer. Every day as she knelt to meditate on the life of Christ, the sister behind her made a constant, low clicking noise, possibly with her rosary beads. It completely distracted Therese, who had sensitive ears. Over and over she fought to bring her mind back to Jesus. The more she tried to ignore the noise, the louder it seemed to grow. It saturated her mind. Therese knitted her brows and glanced from side to side. The other sisters remained still with eyes closed in prayer or books of meditations in their hands. The noise perturbed her alone.

Therese wanted to turn and stare at the offending nun. Then at least she would be aware of the problem. But Therese restrained herself. She did not want to sin against charity. What could she do? This precious hour speaking with her Lord was slipping away amid frustration. Sweat broke out on her forehead and ran down her back.

Then she had an idea. Since she could not ignore the sound, she would make it her prayer. She would offer it to the Lord. "Infant Jesus," she prayed inwardly, "I know children enjoy music. Here is a little symphony for you, a symphony of a bride of Christ at prayer. Let us listen to it together." This trick transformed the noise into a work of art.

Sr. Marie of St. Joseph was another nun who challenged Therese. She suffered from anger and depression. Everyone avoided her as much as they could. In the laundry she repeatedly splashed Therese with dirty water as they washed their clothes in the old-fashioned way. Therese forced herself not to draw back or look annoyed. She resolved to view the water as a blessing, like the holy water the priest sprinkles on the people during the Easter season. The splashes became treasures she could offer to God.

Therese was not the only recipient of Marie of St. Joseph's baptisms. She begged her fellow nuns to pity this sister, who had so many trials and could not help her temperament (HF 241). Therese volunteered to help her mend clothes. They worked side by side for fourteen months, until Therese's health compelled her to quit. A few weeks later she wrote in her autobiography, "This year, God gave me the grace to understand what love is" (TL 281). Many authorities believe she was speaking about Marie of St. Joseph. This poor nun had to leave the convent permanently in 1909 when her depression grew worse.

Perhaps the most amazing relationship in Therese's life was with Sr. Therese of St. Augustine. All the nuns considered this sister abrasive and hard to bear. She openly criticized others. Gorres calls her "sharp, stupid, and conceited" (HF 243). Therese sought her out at recreation and bestowed her most beautiful smiles upon her. Everyone—including Therese of St. Augustine herself—thought the two were best friends. Marie of the Sacred Heart was jealous. How could Therese love another nun more than the sisters who had raised her?

Unknown to anyone, Therese of St. Augustine tried Therese's patience as much as she did everyone else's. Therese prayed for her companion every time they met, and conquered her aversion and annoyance by reminding God of all the nun's virtues. Still, sometimes she ran away when the temptation to answer back sinfully was too strong.

Her sisters were shocked to read in *Story of a Soul* how much effort this relationship cost her. Therese did not reveal the name of the nun who caused her so many struggles, but everyone understood who she was, except Therese of St. Augustine herself. She testified at the investigation into the saint's life that she and Therese of the Child Jesus were particularly close. Years after *Story of a Soul* was published, she still thought the text was talking about somebody else. She remained convinced that Therese was especially attracted to her.

Imagine viewing the annoyances of our days not as personal affronts, but as gifts we can give to Jesus with love! Or seeing them as gifts from him, given with care at just the right place and time to increase our trust in his providence! Imagine showering special affection on those we find it hardest to endure. Is this even possible?

Therese left us two helps she did not have—her example to encourage us and her prayers from heaven to aid us. We can triumph as she did if we ask for her intercession. But this cannot happen unless we are willing. Are we ready to conquer ourselves at every turn, shunning laziness and excuses?

Trust and negative emotions

What does all this have to do with trusting God? Throughout her years as a nun, Therese was refining her spirituality into what we now know as the little way. Six weeks before her death, she summarized it in this manner:

> It is to recognize our nothingness, to expect everything from God as a little child expects everything from his father; it is to be disquieted about nothing and not to be set on gaining our living. . . . Finally, it is not to become discouraged over one's little faults, for children fall often, but they are too little to hurt themselves very much. (LC 138–39)

We have already talked about acknowledging that our virtues come from God. Our next chapter discusses not being discouraged over our faults. In this chapter we will consider another aspect of the little way: being "disquieted about nothing." We'll examine anger's relationship with trust and the role it has played in my life. We'll see how the little way provides a shortcut on the road to heaven.

Miriam-Webster.com lists the following among its synonyms for *disquiet*: agitate, alarm, bother, concern, derail, discomfort, dismay, distress, frazzle, fuss, perturb, unsettle, upset, and worry. How often do our circumstances affect us in these ways? Being disquieted demonstrates a lack of trust.

Therese echoes the teaching of her patron saint, Teresa of Avila, who wrote on a bookmark she kept in her breviary, "Let *nothing* disturb you . . ." (emphasis mine).

Making this teaching more concrete, we might say: If pro-abortionists and opponents of true marriage take over every government office in the land, we will not worry. If we lose our jobs, we will not be upset. If we are diagnosed with cancer, that will not unsettle us. If our computer crashes in the middle of an important blog post, that will not frazzle our nerves. If a violent storm is approaching our city, we will not be alarmed. If we spend the entire day disciplining disobedient children, we will not be agitated. If an author writing about trust brushes aside our legitimate concerns as though they are nothing, we will not be frustrated!

I am not talking about the first movements of emotion. Neither were Therese or Teresa. God built human emotions into our minds and bodies. They move us to protect ourselves and our loved ones, or to support those who are hurting. Jesus himself got angry, and we know he never sinned. So what does not being disquieted really mean?

Here is the Church's teaching about the passions:

> The principal passions are love and hatred, desire and fear, joy, sadness, and anger. In the passions, as movements of the sensitive appetite, there is neither moral good nor evil. But insofar as they engage reason and will, there is moral good or evil in them. (CCC 1772–73)

Let's examine that more closely. Of the passions it speaks of, hatred, fear, sadness, and anger can especially disquiet us. If we wish to follow the little way of trusting God, we will have to be particularly careful in these areas. Passions or emotions can be used for good or for evil. We must choose how we will respond to them.

In a later chapter we will discuss fear and sadness in more detail. Here we will focus on how anger can keep us from trusting God.

We often feel impatient when things don't go our way. Almost immediately we must decide what to do with that feeling. Is there a good act we should perform? A bad act we should avoid?

For example, if I walk into the living room and see that one of the kids has left a toy on the floor in violation of our family rules, I could react in various ways. Initially, my reason might react negatively to the room being out of order. My will might feel distaste at it. This is the first movement of anger. I could choose to ignore the feeling, deciding that my toddler was probably the culprit and it is a small enough offense that I will let it pass. In that case, I let my anger go without acting further.

Or I could see that one of my older boys was at fault and let my anger move me to discipline him. I might have him clean the entire room as punishment. In this case, I use my anger to modify his behavior. It is my responsibility to do so as his mother. My anger then helps me accomplish something good.

At that point, I must recognize that my anger has served its purpose and let it go. If I continue thinking about the incident, I risk nursing the anger. Willfully hanging onto it would be wrong. What would be the purpose?

I could also choose at the start to yell at my son. While yelling may not be sinful itself, it is getting awfully close. It may add fuel to my emotions, so that I find myself criticizing my son's character, or bemoaning the fact that he "never" obeys me. I move from dealing objectively with a problem to feeling personally affronted or personally affronting him. My anger is starting to get out of control. Again I am at fault.

The other passions work in a similar way.

St. Paul writes, "Be angry but do not sin; do not let the sun go down on your anger" (Eph 4:26). He acknowledges that anger is not always sinful. But it is difficult for us fallen human beings to control our passions.

Original Sin affects us, even after our Baptism. Our passions can overtake our reason. The saints advise avoiding anger completely, because we can't easily control it.

Jesus had no stain of Original Sin. When he got angry at the money changers in the Temple (see Mt 21:12–13), his anger was righteous and under the complete control of his reason. As God, he was the rightful judge of those who were defiling God's house.

When we give way to anger, we are often taking over God's role. We seek to punish those who have wronged us, or at least cut them down to size. Now, of course, some people deserve and require temporal punishment. Governments must punish criminals to preserve our safety. Parents must discipline their children to teach them that actions have consequences. But neither government officials nor parents should act out of unbridled anger or revenge. They must, as far as possible, remain objective and deal out discipline or punishment for the good of the offender, and of the family or society. Their emotions can move them to discipline, but must be guided by reason so that punishments remain just. And those of us not in positions of authority should leave punishing offenders to those who are, and to God.

If we truly trust God, we will not try to rule in his place. We will not be personally offended by others' bad behavior. St. Paul says, "Beloved, never avenge yourselves, but leave it to the wrath of God; for it is written, 'Vengeance is mine, I will repay, says the Lord'" (Rom 12:19).

Struggling against anger

I have always had trouble controlling my temper. I grew up thinking that anger itself—not just some expressions of it—was sinful. This is a common misunderstanding of Catholic teaching. We know that anger is one of the seven capital sins, but we don't always hear that it is *willed* anger, not the first movement of the passion, that is often sinful.

As a child, I had violent bursts of temper, lashing out at the brothers who were closest in age to me. But as I grew older, I worked on controlling my anger. I had experienced aggressive, hurtful anger from both sides, but had seen few examples of anger being handled properly. So I saw only two alternatives. I could be angry, which was sinful. Or I could righteously reject anger. But we cannot always avoid feeling the passions. When I tried to do so, I was actually suppressing my anger.

I became so used to suppressing it that I did not even know when I was angry. By my late teens, I thought my anger problem was past. I rarely expressed any anger with my peers. I even told others that God had healed me of my anger. I could not have been more wrong.

Parenting brought out my anger in disturbing ways. Dan and I had three sons in the first five years of our marriage. Since I had spent so many years caring for younger brothers and a sister, I thought I understood what parenting would be like. I knew how to change diapers, make formula and baby cereal, dress an infant, and rock him to sleep. But babysitting is a far cry from parenting. I had never been up all night with a child, never missed a shower because I had no time for it.

Having Dante was culture shock! Dan and I entered a foreign land. Every daily routine was different. Instead of our being the ones in control of our lives, our infant sat in the executive's chair.

Dante greeted the world with a scream. Now I knew why I felt him move in the womb so early. He had explosive energy. He hated to sleep. From the time we came home from the hospital until he was nearly two, brief snoozes after eating were his only naps. If we moved while holding him or tried to put him down, he instantly awoke.

One day a family friend whose children were grown visited us. Exclaiming over Dante, she asked, "Don't you just love him more than you ever thought possible?"

"Uh—yeah," I replied shamefacedly. Of course, I did love him, because love is a matter of will, not only of feelings. I will forever thank God for that distinction. I was too stunned and sleep-deprived at that time to feel anything.

Two children later, I appreciated the early days of my children's lives much more. I was no longer a parenting novice. But neither was I a perfect mom. I kept waiting for life to get easier, for more time to myself, more quiet, more control of my days—or at least more sleep!

Fr. Groeschel says that when a crisis strikes, people often return to their childhood habits in reacting to it, especially if they have unresolved issues, as I did with trust (SP 41). As I strove to parent my children, I was surprised and dismayed to see the bad habits of childhood reappearing. Through no fault of their own, my children brought out the worst in me. I often yelled at my boys or otherwise did not discipline them in love. Peace eluded our home and my heart.

My lack of self-control concerned me. Where was the sanctity I was striving for?

Being an avid reader, I bought some books on managing anger. My reading taught me that frustration, impatience, irritability, and feelings of futility were all manifestations of anger. I realized I was angry at other adults often, but had never recognized that anger. And I saw that, as a mother, I was angry nearly all the time! That knowledge discouraged me.

How distrust relates to anger

Like distrust, chronic anger is often rooted in childhood. Not all causes of anger relate to trust, but some definitely do. According to bestselling author Dr. Les Carter, anger is almost always a response to feeling controlled. People who misuse their anger seek to take back control of a difficult situation (*The Anger Trap*. San Francisco: Jossey-Bass, 2003, 59).

Some people, including me, hide their anger as one way to regain control. We think other people can't have power over us if they remain in the dark about our feelings (ibid., 59–60). I also hide my anger because I believe others will condemn me if I express it. Then I feel that others control when and how I can express my emotions. That in turn leads me to greater anger. I also set myself up for further problems. Though the main point of my suppressing how I feel is disguising my true self, I have often complained that everyone misinterprets my character. People cannot get to know me if I refuse to let them.

If I trusted that others would accept me no matter what, I could express my emotions freely. If I saw everything in my life as under God's providential care, I could learn to embrace my circumstances. Instead, I live as though I am a puppet animated by other people and conditions outside myself. I feel helpless to manage my anger, because I can't manage the details of my life.

But I was never meant to!

We are not the gods of our lives. We will never rule over every detail. Circumstances beyond our control remind us that God alone holds our lives in his hands. These circumstances call us to surrender to him.

Other angry people snatch at control in different ways. Some display aggression, forcing their opponents to hear them out. Others withdraw or use manipulation.

Chronically angry people often depend on others for their sense of self-worth. They expect others to support, encourage, and agree with them. They look for security in creatures rather than in their Creator. When others disagree with them, they feel threatened. They see disagreement as disapproval, and they take that disapproval to heart.

Our self-worth comes from God alone. He created us in his image and likeness. He made us to share his life and love with us. Jesus suffered and died to make this possible. We need to accept our essential worth that comes from God and stop worrying about what others think of us. Their judgment cannot affect our eternal destiny.

A further group of people has anger that stems from pride. Placing their trust in themselves, they belittle and oppose others at every turn. They can't stand to be contradicted, because they are always right about everything. They need to learn humility. They need to acknowledge that they do not speak for God. I certainly have some of this type of anger too.

Trusting in God's goodness is not just for life's tragedies. God also calls us to trust him in our vocations and in the little frustrations of daily life. He manifests his providence there as well. "God is in the details," from being splashed with dirty water to changing dirty diapers. From the nun who disturbs our mental prayer to the co-worker who disturbs our computer programming.

Therese looked for the good in Sr. Therese of St. Augustine. Can we look for the good in unpleasant situations as well? Can we persevere when the good masks itself? As St. John of the Cross, whose works she devoutly read, wrote, "Where there is no love, put love and you will draw out love" (*The Collected Work of St. John of the Cross,* translated by Kieran Kavanaugh, OCD and Otilio Rodriguez, OCD. Washington, DC: ICS Publications, 1991, 760). If we can find no good in our situation, let us *become* the good in it. Pouting or raging won't accomplish this.

We cannot control every facet of our lives, but we can take ownership of them. We can embrace our irritations out of love for God, transforming them into a ladder towards heaven.

Then again, who needs a ladder, when Therese offers us an elevator?

An elevator to holiness

Therese explained her discovery of the little way of spiritual childhood to Mother Agnes in this way:

> I wanted to find an elevator which would raise me to Jesus, for I am too small to climb the rough stairway of perfection. I searched, then, in the Scriptures for some sign of this elevator, the object of my desires, and I read these words coming from the mouth of Eternal Wisdom: *"Whoever is a LITTLE ONE, let him come to me"* [Prv 9:4]. And so I succeeded. I felt I had found what I was looking for. But wanting to know, O my God, what You would do to *the very little one* who answered Your call, I continued my search and this is what I discovered: *"As one whom a mother caresses, so will I comfort you; you shall be carried at the breasts, and upon the knees they shall caress you"* [Is 66:13, 12]. . . . The elevator which must raise me to heaven is Your arms, O Jesus! (SS 207–8, emphasis in the original)

Jesus is the ladder or stairway to heaven (see Gn 28 and Jn 1:50–51). He is our way to salvation. As both God and man, he is the means to man's union with God. He is the means, and he is also the end.

We can think of the stairway to heaven in two ways. It symbolizes not only our salvation—the ability to enter heaven, but also our justification—the process of being made holy. A stairway from the beginnings of the spiritual life to sainthood could take eons to climb. Without extraordinary help, few people would reach the top.

What about weak, ordinary people? How could we fulfill our destiny—for God made us all to be saints?

Therese wrote: "Oh Jesus, *your little bird* is happy to be *weak and little.* What would become of it if it were big?" (SS 199, emphasis in the original). Weakness did not deter her, it made her more confident. She said that "God cannot inspire unrealizable desires" (SS 207). So if God inspired her to become a saint, he would make the way. If she had no merits to help her climb to the heights of holiness, God would do all the work. He would be her elevator. All she needed to do was entrust herself totally to him.

"I feel that if You found a soul weaker and littler than mine, which is impossible, You would be pleased to grant it still greater favors, provided it abandoned itself with total confidence to Your Infinite Mercy" (SS 200).

Are we weaker than Therese by nature? Only God can answer that question. In the early stages of following God, it's difficult for us to understand how weak we are. We think we can do anything, now that we've decided to follow him. We don't understand why the people around us are still struggling with sin. We grow impatient with them. We judge them for their abrasive personalities or annoying habits. We imagine we are so strong!

But we will not become saints that way. We need to acknowledge our weakness and littleness and see them as assets, not detriments, to holiness. The littler we are, the easier it is for Jesus to pick us up and carry us.

Whether we struggle with anger, fear, sadness, or worry, each gives us the opportunity to own our need for God. Each time we are tempted by uncharitable thoughts about someone, or wish we could avoid them altogether, we have an opportunity to grow in humility and trust.

Let us embrace the trials of our daily lives, but not in order to earn merits for heaven, or with an eye to becoming great. Let us embrace them because they are part of God's providential plan for us. We can abandon ourselves to that plan. We can trust that, as Jesus promised, nothing can harm us, as long as we place ourselves in his arms (see Lk 10:19).

Questions for Reflection

1. What sinful habits in my life betray a lack of trust? Am I anxious, angry, depressed, or distraught? Am I overly concerned about my weaknesses?

2. What normal occurrences tend to destroy my peace of mind? Am I willing to accept them if God allows them to happen? Can I at least try to see them as gifts?

Practical Suggestions

* If your spouse, parents, boss, or others in your life are burdening you with unrealistic expectations, find a way to talk to them about it. Pray for peace and wisdom first. Speak to them when neither one of you is emotional. Be ready with suggestions for more realistic goals. Speak honestly, but respectfully and listen attentively to their response.

* Pray for the grace to be open to God's will at every moment.

* At the end of each day, thank God for the many blessings he sent, even if it was a day of struggle. Thank him especially for the times you overcame temptation, and the times you successfully trusted in him rather than in yourself.

Chapter Eight
A Way for the Weak and Sinful

I tell you, there will be more joy in heaven over one sinner who repents than over ninety-nine righteous persons who need no repentance.

Lk 15:7

Therese never had a consistent spiritual director. In the beginning, she longed for one. When she was suffering from scruples as a teen, a director could have reassured her about her spiritual state. God's plan for her excluded that consolation.

Marie and Celine had long submitted to the direction of Fr. Pichon, a Jesuit and a family friend. Shortly after Therese entered into Carmel, Fr. Pichon came to witness Marie's profession of vows. The evening before the ceremony, he joined the nuns for mental prayer. He noticed the peaceful way Therese went about her prayer. He smiled to himself. *A young, idealistic girl*, he thought. *How beautiful the spiritual life of the young is, before the soul has any real problems!*

Therese worked hard to maintain her peaceful expression at prayer. She was struggling against another onset of scruples. Her first three months in Carmel were some of the happiest in her life. But now she began second-guessing herself. She made a general confession, telling Fr. Pichon about her early vocation, her scruples, her Christmas conversion, and her attitude since entering the cloister.

Her depth and her struggles surprised Fr. Pichon. He had also overcome scruples. Rejecting the Jansenism of many of his fellow priests, he brought comfort and encouragement to sinners through his preaching and direction.

As Therese placed her life and spirituality before the priest, God granted her a gift she would never forget. Fr. Pichon solemnly swore that she had never committed a mortal sin. He also reminded her that God's grace had protected her. "Thank God for what He has done for you," he said. "Had He abandoned you, instead of being a little angel, you would have become a little demon" (SS 149). Therese's spirits soared. He was confirming everything she believed.

Fr. Pichon directed Therese for only a brief time. He sailed for the missions of Canada a few months after her general confession. He exchanged some letters with her over the years, but for the most part, his direction was over. But his influence on her spirituality endured.

Therese learned during her years of constant scrupulosity not to focus on her merits. When Fr. Pichon confirmed that she had never gravely sinned, she could have fallen into the opposite and worse error of pride. She may have had a natural tendency towards the type of pride that expects too much of oneself (see HF 57). But she knew by now to rely on God's grace for everything.

The little way suits sinners

People love to say how normal Therese was. She did not experience many supernatural phenomena. She shows us that these are unnecessary for sanctity. She gives us hope that anyone can be a saint.

But in one significant way, Therese was definitely not "normal." Few of us can truthfully say we have never committed mortal sin. Reading about Therese's innocence, we face a new temptation. We look at all of our sins and wonder, *How can I even relate to a saint like this?*

In this chapter we'll discover how sinners can trust fully in God, following the example of the Penitent Woman in the Gospels. We'll learn of

Therese's special love for penitents. I will share how I repeatedly failed in my spiritual life, and how these failures were actually a blessing.

We err if we think that Therese never struggled against sin. She must have bitten her tongue a thousand times in her relations with other nuns. She knew what self-conquest meant. Later she would endure doubt and darkness that we can barely imagine. We can apply this biblical passage about Jesus to her as well: "For because he himself has suffered and been tempted, he is able to help those who are tempted" (Heb 2:18).

Therese always loved sinners. A home for former prostitutes run by the Sisters of Our Lady of Mercy in Lisieux captured her imagination as an adolescent. Two hundred young women filled its dormitories. The sisters welcomed them for as long as they wanted to stay, teaching them trades and extending God's mercy to them. Some discerned a vocation and joined the order.

Louis Martin often brought fish to the Refuge, as it was called. Therese sometimes accompanied him. She daydreamed about hiding herself among the penitents, letting no one know that she was not a converted fallen woman. Afterwards, she mused, she could join the order and minister to the other penitents.

Before she embraced Carmel's vocation of praying for priests, she showed her love for sinners in another way. She prayed and offered sacrifices for them.

The Martin family taught Therese about God's infinite mercy—not just with words, but with action. Whenever as a child she disobeyed and was reprimanded, she immediately repented. Then she experienced total forgiveness. No one reminded her of her past faults. No one held onto bitterness or resentment (see HF 52).

The Carmel of Lisieux had a corner grotto, a solitary place to pray known as the Hermitage of St. Mary Magdalene. Therese spoke and wrote of this penitent saint a surprising amount, given the differences in their lives. Her interest reached the level of devotion. One year she received a particular grace while praying in the hermitage. She felt like she was covered with the Virgin Mary's veil for days, and went about her tasks as though someone else was performing them.

At another time she wrote to Fr. Belliere, a missionary priest she was praying for and encouraging,

> When I see [St. Mary] Magdalene walking up before the many guests, washing with her tears the feet of her adored Master, whom she is touching for the first time, I feel that her heart has understood the abysses of love and mercy of the Heart of Jesus. (STL 14)

Therese also wrote that in her spiritual life she ran to take the lowest place at Jesus' banquet table, imitating Mary Magdalene rather than the Pharisee.

> Her astonishing or rather her loving audacity which charms the Heart of Jesus also attracts my own. . . . Even though I had on my conscience all the sins that can be committed, I would go, my heart broken with sorrow, and throw myself into Jesus' arms. (SS 258–59)

And regarding her innocence, she said that "the profound words of Our Lord to Simon resound with a great sweetness in my soul," when she realized how much she depended on God's grace (SS 83). What were these consoling words? Here is the story:

> One of the Pharisees asked him to eat with him, and he went into the Pharisee's house, and took his place at table. And behold, a woman of the city, who was a sinner,

> when she learned that he was at table in the Pharisee's house, brought an alabaster flask of ointment, and standing behind him at his feet, weeping, she began to wet his feet with her tears, and wiped them with the hair of her head, and kissed his feet, and anointed them with the ointment. Now when the Pharisee who had invited him saw it, he said to himself, "If this man were a prophet, he would have known who and what sort of woman this is who is touching him, for she is a sinner." (Lk 7:36–39)

The woman in this passage, though not named, is traditionally linked with Mary Magdalene and Mary of Bethany. I am sympathetic to the tradition and think the Bible lends it support, but many modern scholars are skeptical of it. Since some dispute this identification, I will call the woman in this passage the Penitent Woman, while Therese calls her St. Mary Magdalene.

The story continues:

> And Jesus answering said to him, "Simon, I have something to say to you." And he answered, "What is it, Teacher?" "A certain creditor had two debtors; one owed five hundred denarii, and the other fifty. When they could not pay, he forgave them both. Now which of them will love him more?" Simon answered, "The one, I suppose, to whom he forgave more." And he said to him, "You have judged rightly." Then turning toward the woman he said to Simon, "Do you see this woman? I entered your house, you gave me no water for my feet, but she has wet my feet with her tears and wiped them with her hair. You gave me no kiss, but from the time I came in she has not ceased to kiss my feet. You did not

> anoint my head with oil, but she has anointed my feet with ointment. Therefore I tell you, her sins, which are many, are forgiven, for she loved much; but he who is forgiven little, loves little." And he said to her, "Your sins are forgiven." Then those who were at table with him began to say among themselves, "Who is this, who even forgives sins?" And he said to the woman, "Your faith has saved you; go in peace." (Lk 7:40–50)

Who loves God more?

The Penitent Woman had committed many mortal sins that were known publicly. God forgave her much. Therese, on the other hand, had few sins for God to forgive. We could assume after reading this story that the Penitent Woman loved God more than Therese did. Therese did not accept this judgment.

Yes, God had forgiven the Penitent Woman much. But that was only half the story. "He wants me *to love* Him because He *has forgiven* me not much but ALL," Therese wrote. "He has not expected me to *love Him much* like Mary Magdalene, but He has willed that I know how He has loved me in advance with a love of *unspeakable foresight*, in order that now I may love Him unto folly" (SS 84, emphasis in the original).

In 1850, Pope Pius IX defined the doctrine of the Immaculate Conception. Therese knew it well. God applied the merits of Christ's death and Resurrection to the Blessed Virgin Mary from the moment of her conception in order to preserve her from every sin. In a similar, though lesser, way, Therese believed God had protected her from falling into mortal sin. God acted to preserve her innocence before she could act to compromise it.

Since infancy, she practiced strict adherence to the truth. Looking back on her childhood, she saw her nature clearly enough that, as Gorres says, she knew "goodness is a gift, is grace, freely conferred apart from all deserving, by God's mercy and unfathomable choice" (HF 59).

Therese had brilliant insight into the Gospel passage about the Penitent Woman. People who have always followed Jesus do not necessarily love him less than converted sinners. Where would that leave his mother? Did the Virgin Mary love God least of all, since she did not even bear the stain of Original Sin? How absurd! She loved him most.

What did Jesus mean, then? He was criticizing those who rely on themselves for righteousness and think themselves good apart from grace. Presumably Simon the Pharisee was such a person. His love for God was small compared to those who realize that they are totally dependent on God's goodness. He was like the unnamed Pharisee we talked about in chapter 5, who praised himself before God.

Many of us start life in Christ with an inflated image of ourselves. We hope in our strength, rather than God's. When we finally recognize our unworthiness, we are tempted instead to despair. Our faults appear greater than our virtues. But this need not trouble us.

Even those of us with a particularly sinful past have no reason to despair of God's love. The Penitent Woman is the model for sinners.

Like Therese, the Penitent Woman had no illusions about herself. No one had to tell her she had messed up her life. No one had to tell her she could not get to heaven on her merits. When she learned how loving, merciful, and understanding God was, she poured out not only her perfume, but her entire life for Jesus. She opened her heart to receive his love and forgiveness.

Therese needed God as much as the Penitent Woman did. She did nothing to deserve the graces he had given her, and she embraced this knowledge. What merit was there in not giving in to sins that never tempted her? Her only merit was being open to grace—the same merit the Penitent Woman displayed. Both followed the promptings of the

Holy Spirit in their hearts. Both trusted totally in Jesus.

Here I might pose the same rhetorical question John C. H. Wu asks in his book, *The Science of Love: a Study in the Teachings of Therese of Lisieux*. "But why have I dwelt so long upon Mary Magdalene?" I would answer the way he did as well. "Because she is the prototype of Therese of Lisieux. She knew the art of love. Having given all, she feels as though she had given nothing" (http://www.ewtn.com/library/spirit/sci-love.txt).

Both sinners and those who have been saints since childhood must follow the same general path to God. We all journey on the same narrow way. Neither the Penitent Woman's sinful past nor Therese's innocent past would determine how great a saint each would be, but only their absolute trust in God. Here we come back to the words of Therese that we quoted at the beginning. "It is trust, and nothing but trust, that must bring us to Love."

Sinners have nothing to fear from God, as long as they repent. He is always merciful, "slow to anger, and abounding in steadfast love, forgiving iniquity and transgression" (Nm 4:18). The Lord does not want to punish sinners, but to redeem them. Our Savior came to earth for this purpose. He reserves his harsh words for the self-righteous. And even if we have been self-righteous in the past, we can still repent and find mercy.

We can learn to trust God like the Penitent Woman. We can learn to trust God like Therese.

How should we react when we sin?

A sinner who comes to God in repentance and commits his life to Christ is a beautiful thing. But what happens after our initial conversion? Inevitably we fall into sin. How should we as Christians react when we sin? Shouldn't we anguish over our trespasses, when we have failed such a loving Lord?

What does our expert on trust say? In a letter to her sister Celine after she herself had entered Carmel, Therese writes, "I am not always faithful, but I never get discouraged; I abandon myself into the arms of Jesus" (EW 76).

Like the Penitent Woman who threw herself at our Lord's feet, Therese threw herself into our Lord's arms whenever she sinned. Her confidence was not shaken.

The saints all agree that when we sin we should remain calm. This is counter-intuitive. When I first tried to practice not being anxious when I sinned, it felt wrong. I felt like I was making light of my sin. If I did not get angry and upset with myself, was I really serious about following God?

Anger at ourselves when we sin reveals that we are still counting on our own righteousness to save us, rather than on God's mercy and grace. God wants us to repent peacefully, then go on with our lives.

Therese takes this common teaching a step further than others have done. Consider this passage from another of her letters to Fr. Belliere:

> I would like to try to make you understand by means of a very simple comparison how much Jesus loves even imperfect souls who confide in Him: I picture a father who has two children, mischievous and disobedient, and when he comes to punish them, he sees one of them who trembles and gets away from him in terror, having, however, in the bottom of his heart the feeling that he deserves to be punished; and his brother, on the contrary, throws himself into his father's arms, saying that he is sorry for having caused him any trouble, that he loves him, and to prove it he will be good from now on, and if

> this child asked his father *to punish* him with *a kiss*, I do not believe that the heart of the happy father could resist the filial confidence of his child, whose sincerity and love he knows. He realizes, however, that more than once his son will fall into the same faults, but he is prepared to pardon him always, if his son always takes him by the heart. (EW 172–73)

Therese is saying that when we sin, we should trust God so much that we ask him to bless us in place of punishment.

This teaching astonishes me. Human nature says that when we sin, we should run away from God like Adam did. We expect God to reject us, or at least to punish us severely when we come to him in repentance. Even after we have practiced remaining calm when we sin, we still think that our sins have set us back. We confess them and do our penance or otherwise make reparation, but we have a lingering sense that we are out of step with God.

Therese was bold. She did not stop at accepting her sinfulness as part of the human condition. She asked for a kiss from God whenever she sinned.

We can do the same.

Now, granted, our sins are probably worse than hers. So were the Penitent Woman's. But if we are Christians, our God is exactly the same as hers. That's the point.

Do we expect to earn heaven by being good, or to be rewarded with what we don't deserve? If we despair because we have sinned, or think that we have no call to trust God as much as Therese did, we must remember the Penitent Woman. Jesus did not turn her away. Her love and trust won his heart. He defended her against her critics.

Sometimes we are harder on ourselves than Jesus was on repentant sinners. We tell ourselves that, unlike the Penitent Woman, we have long called ourselves Christians. We have claimed to know God, to be his children. We have had the Holy Trinity living in our hearts since our Baptism. We have actual grace and the grace of the sacraments to keep us from sin. So we have no excuse.

We have no excuse for failing to trust God, would be Therese's response, I believe.

Pride is the most ancient sin. It is the worst of the capital sins. Like the Devil who committed the first sin of pride, it is sly. It conceals itself under numerous cloaks of virtue in order to bring us down.

Pride is obvious when we think our virtues gain us God's favor. But it's also at work when we fear that the sins we are truly sorry for keep us distant from him. In both cases, we are focusing too much on ourselves. Our focus should be on God. We must keep our eyes on his strength and goodness.

We trust God, not because *we* are good, but because *he* is. The more we trust him, the more he will prove himself trustworthy. Our sins are not too big for God. Our trust is too little.

Of course, we cannot be presumptuous, only pretending to repent without resolving to do better in the future. Presumption is a sin. If we presume that God will overlook our mortal sins, or forgive them without the aid of the Sacrament of Reconciliation, then our presumption itself is mortally sinful. It will never win us a kiss from God. But neither should we despair, no matter what we have done, no matter how many times we have fallen. Our sins do not change God.

God works for our good *in all things*—even our sins. We can make this true in our lives by asking God to draw us closer to him every time we sin.

My persistent failure

As I said at the start of this book, several years ago I got stuck in my spiritual life. There were many reasons for that. One was pride. Another was a lack of trust.

God answered my prayers about becoming more humble when I had kids. The return of my anger problem (more accurately, the revelation that the problem had never been resolved) helped me to see myself more realistically.

Waking up on a typical morning, I prayed, "God, please help me to handle my anger in a Christian way today. Help me make some progress." I was determined to count on God's grace and to practice the anger-management techniques I had read about.

The first few hours of the day went well. *Maybe this is becoming a habit*, I thought. *I'm going to overcome this after all.* One of the boys talked back to me, and I felt the first movements of anger. *Why is this making me angry?* I asked myself as I had learned. I recognized that I didn't like to be defied because it threatened my self-worth. I was basing my self-image on the behavior of those around me. When my kids questioned me, I questioned myself, not just as a parent, but as a human being. *My self-worth comes from God,* I mentally repeated. *I can let this anger go.*

But as the day wore on, reason and resistance waned. Lunch was the hardest time of day. Dan came home from work to join us. I felt the pressure of having to serve him right away so that within half an hour he could be back at work. At the same time, Michael, our toddler, asked for a piece of cheese, and Dante, then three, spilled his juice. I lost it. I yelled at both boys as though they were acting out on purpose.

Instantly, guilt and frustration poured over me. I had failed again. What kind of a mother was I? What kind of a Christian? Why wasn't I getting any better at this?

I couldn't put the brakes on my anger. The first blowup left me twisted up inside, setting the stage for the second, and the third. Anger triggers followed one another so rapidly that I didn't have time to work through each one. For the rest of the day, I yelled more often than I talked.

Focusing on overcoming it took almost all my mental energy. I was expecting our third child at that time, so I had little energy to spare. I went to bed exhausted and depressed.

This pattern repeated itself day after day, month after month, year after year. Create high ideals. Try to meet them. Fail. It seemed like there was no way out of this cycle.

Finally, I asked my brother, a Carmelite monk, to pray for me. Then I decided to concentrate on other issues, because I just did not see how I could win this battle.

The gift of failure

God gives us the grace of failure to teach us to rely only on him alone. Therese experienced this with her over-sensitive nature. She also had another experience of failure.

When the Virgin of the Smile cured her of her illness in 1883, Therese made up her mind to keep the miracle a secret. Only she, God, and the Blessed Virgin would know it. She felt that all the joy of the cure would disappear with the revelation of it. But Marie guessed that something extraordinary had happened, and Therese found herself telling her about it. Marie in turn told the Carmelite nuns on their next visit to see Sr. Agnes. The nuns quizzed Therese about it, assuming she had a vision like those they had read about in saints' stories. Her answers did not fit their preconceived notions of what a grace from the Virgin would be like. Their clear disappointment made Therese wonder if she had lied about the incident. Had she just made it up? If only she would have remained silent!

God allows us to fail also to rid us of our pride. We can learn to see our failures as a grace, a means of salvation.

St. Paul experienced this too:

> To keep me from being too elated by the abundance of revelations, a thorn was given me in the flesh, a messenger of Satan, to harass me, to keep me from being too elated. Three times I besought the Lord about this, that it should leave me; but he said to me, "My grace is sufficient for you, for my power is made perfect in weakness." I will all the more gladly boast of my weaknesses, that the power of Christ may rest upon me. For the sake of Christ, then, I am content with weaknesses, insults, hardships, persecutions, and calamities; for when I am weak, then I am strong. (2 Cor 12:7–10)

Before we can become strong in Christ, we must recognize our weakness. God allows us as Christians to sin, even to sin miserably at times, in order to bring about a higher good. Even Adam's sin has been called a "happy fault" (*felix culpa* in Latin), because the result of his sin was Christ's coming as a man for our salvation.

This does not mean we treat sin lightly or cease fighting temptation. On the contrary, we fight it more than ever, but do so peacefully. And when we fail, as we will at some point, we retain our peace. God often, if not always, brings us to a place of powerlessness so that we will learn to trust him rather than ourselves. He did that for me in letting me set up expectations for myself that I could never meet. I had to fail over and over before my eyes were opened.

Homeschooling my older sons while our fourth was an infant was especially trying for me. Again my anger came to the fore. It was the first year I was homeschooling three children at once. I had a kindergartner, a second grader, and a fourth grader. The last time I had an infant, Dante was in kindergarten and I was teaching about an hour a day. That was easy to fit into our life, in short spurts. Now our school day was lasting from nine to two.

The first few months after John Mark's birth, he was the best sleeper I had (which isn't saying much). But at four months old, he suddenly stopped napping, besides regressing in his nighttime sleep habits. He interrupted every lesson, often multiple times. We were constantly behind. If any of my older sons caused problems, he'd better watch out! I sometimes yelled myself hoarse. Then I developed digestive problems, at least partly due to stress.

Although I am completely committed to homeschooling my boys until high school graduation if possible, I considered putting them in school for sanity's sake. Ultimately, I made some changes to the way we ran our school day so that someone was always giving John Mark the attention he needed. Thankfully, the next school year went more smoothly.

But I would still fall into the pattern of stress and anger from time to time. Reading *The Way of Trust and Love* by Fr. Jacques Philippe opened my eyes to the solution. When he quoted Therese's letter about asking God for a kiss, I was dumbfounded. How different my response to sin had always been! I decided to do as the son in Therese's story had done. I started asking God for a kiss as my punishment, an increase in grace and closeness to him every time I sinned. I asked him to draw me even closer than I would have been if I had withstood temptation.

Suddenly, my whole attitude about life changed. I began to find a peace that had been missing. I felt so much freer. Asking for a kiss became routine. I still have bad days of yelling at my kids or otherwise being selfish, but I no longer scold myself for it. I trust God to take care of it, and even to bless me—not because of my sin, but because of his goodness.

I realized that for years in the confessional I had been giving lip service to the same reality when I said, "Bless me, Father, for I have sinned." Not, "Bless me because my sins merit me a blessing," but, "Bless me because I need it, because I am totally dependent on God for strength."

My faith and hope are stronger now as well. I recognized that distress over the lack of progress in my spiritual life was leading me to doubt God's goodness. I was not seeing his promises come to fruition in me, so I began to doubt those promises, instead of trusting in him no matter how things appeared.

Focusing on trust does not cause the same problems for me that focusing on anger did. For one thing, I am looking at life from a positive, rather than a negative, angle. I am trying to increase my trust, rather than just overcome my anger. But more importantly, I have found that nearly everything in life can be viewed from the standpoint of trust. I can apply it to every temptation, every disappointment, every fear. I don't need to analyze the causes of my anger in each situation. I just trustfully give my situation to Jesus, no matter what it is. Trust is a comprehensive way to advance in my spiritual life.

When my little one is naughty, he sometimes lays his curly head on my shoulder and says, "Sorry, Mom." Then he looks at me with his big blue eyes, adds, "I like you," and kisses my whole face. How can I punish him when he does that? I make myself give him a timeout for his own good. But I cannot stay angry at him or resist kissing him back. Neither can God resist bestowing his love and grace on us when we come to him repentant and full of trust. He is our Father. He has no desire to punish us, but to shower undeserved gifts upon us.

> For you did not receive the spirit of slavery to fall back into fear, but you have received the spirit of sonship. When we cry, "Abba! Father!" it is the Spirit himself bearing witness with our spirit that we are children of God, and if children, then heirs, heirs of God and fellow heirs with Christ, provided we suffer with him in order that we may also be glorified with him (Rom 8:15–17).

Do we dare to live in the spirit of sonship? Do we dare to accept our inheritance as children of God?

Questions for Reflection

1. Do I relate to God out of love or fear? Am I too afraid of his displeasure to open up to him fully?

2. Am I in the state of grace? Do I have unconfessed mortal sin or habitual venial sin that is keeping me distant from God?

3. Do I get trapped in a cycle of failure, guilt, and despair?

Practical Suggestions

* Go to the Sacrament of Reconciliation. If it has been a long time since you last went, make an appointment with your parish priest so that neither of you feels rushed. Besides confessing your sins, tell him about your fear and guilt. Let him know you seek to grow in trust and ask his advice.

* Ask God for a kiss whenever you come to him repentant after sinning. Then trust him to bless you and move on. Don't dwell on your fault any longer, unless it is a mortal sin. In that case, confess it as soon as possible (see suggestion above).

Chapter Nine
Facing Our Greatest Fears

There is no fear in love, but perfect love casts out fear.

1 Jn 4:18

Since childhood, Therese feared losing her father more than anything else. He was the one adult in her life who had remained constant. He was her King, her image of God the Father. When she entered the cloister, she died to the world. She knew that it meant leaving loved ones behind. She had visited her sisters in the parlor of the convent for years. Now she was like a bride who had entered her husband's house. No longer so dependent upon her father, she would never be under her his roof again, never go on fishing trips or take walks through the city. Yet, she expected to see him regularly for visits.

God planned a different future for the Martin family. Less than three months after Therese entered Carmel, on June 23, 1888, Louis Martin was missing from home. Most authorities believe he was suffering from end-stage kidney failure, which can result in memory loss, confusion, and cognitive decline. Coupled with this, he was probably suffering from a thickening in the walls of the arteries leading to his brain, which would account for his seizure in 1887, as well as his later paralysis (TL 146).

Leonie was still living at home after her second failed attempt at religious life. She, Celine, and a servant frantically searched the grounds of

Les Buissonnets. They checked to see if Louis had gone to the Guerins' home, but Isidore and his family had not seen Louis. By nightfall there was still no word of him.

The following day, Celine received a letter from Le Havre, a port city over forty miles away. Louis requested her to send him money in care of the post office. He included no return address. He was acting on an impulse to travel to a far off land where he could be a hermit. Instead of sending him anything or answering the letter, Celine Martin, Isidore Guerin, and Celine Guerin's nephew Ernest Maudelonde travelled to Le Havre. They waited for Louis to return to the post office. Celine Guerin stayed in Lisieux, passing letters and telegrams between various family members as they reached her. Leonie, meanwhile, informed the Carmelites of what was happening.

That same day, a house in the Les Buissonnets neighborhood burned to the ground. The roof of Les Buissonnets caught fire. Leonie had to face this situation alone. Thankfully, firemen extinguished the fire before it did extensive damage to the Martin home.

Louis finally returned to the Le Havre post office on June 27. His family brought him home. Thus began the slow degeneration that ended in his death in 1894.

Therese's clothing ceremony was scheduled for October. Louis was supposed to walk her down the aisle like a bride. He suffered another attack in August that made the date uncertain. At last her clothing was rescheduled for January 10, 1889.

Therese had just turned sixteen. Still in many ways a child, she had prayed for snow for her clothing. The day dawned warm. Trying not to give way to disappointment, Therese put on a beautiful dress of white velvet with a sweeping train and the famous Alençon lace. Her golden hair cascaded over her shoulders, crowned with white lilies, a gift from Aunt Celine. A novice's hair was usually cropped a few months after taking the habit.

Therese stepped outside the cloister for the ceremony, at the end of which the nuns would formally receive her again. Louis, father of the bride of Christ, met her at the door. His eyes were misty. "Ah! Here is my little Queen!" he exclaimed (SS 155). He walked her down the aisle of the chapel. Therese's emotions tumbled over one another. How much had changed since her last walk with her father, down the streets of Lisieux! Louis looked peaceful, "handsome," and "dignified" (ibid.). He guided her to the altar, then joined Celine and Leonie, who sat in a pew with the Guerin family. Later, Therese viewed this walk as his glorious entry into Jerusalem, the Palm Sunday before his Passion.

Therese knelt on a special kneeler, holding a lighted candle, while Bishop Hugonin led the congregation in Vespers and gave a short sermon. At the end of the ceremony, he made a mistake, singing the *Te Deum*, when he should have sung the *Veni Creator.*

Then Therese gave her father a final hug, and processed to the cloister door, where the nuns awaited her. To her delight, snow was falling outside!

The nuns completed the ceremony within the cloister walls. In exchange for her wedding attire, Therese donned the Carmelite habit. The brown robe and scapular were made of rough wool. She fastened a close-fitting white cap under her chin. She also wore a white mantle with a wooden clasp and a white veil, the sign that she was not yet a professed member of the order.

This day she put aside her old self and her old life at Les Buissonnets forever. But she did not set aside her concern and affection for her beloved father. Today she added "the Holy Face" to the end of her religious name. During the course of his illness, Louis sometimes hid his face under a towel. The Martin sisters saw this as the fulfillment of Therese's vision of him with his face veiled. Her father's face hidden,

Therese looked "more than ever at the Holy Face of Jesus" (TL 148).

Louis had sent the convent champagne for the celebration, along with an artificial melon that burst open like a piñata and spilled out candy.

Ten days later he had a relapse of his illness. Fearing for his safety and that of the two daughters living with him, he purchased a revolver. Delirium soon overtook him. His daughters put him to bed. He hallucinated about drums and canon fire. Suddenly, he sat up in bed and grabbed his gun. Celine and Leonie could not persuade him to give it up. They sent for their uncle, who came with a friend as quickly as he could and disarmed him.

The doctor suggested that the family confine Louis to a hospital for everyone's sake. A short time later, Isidore and a friend invited Louis out for a walk. They stopped at the convent to give Sr. Agnes a present of freshly caught fish. This was no ordinary walk, however. They led him towards the Bon Sauveur mental hospital in Caen without his knowing the destination. Caen was about thirty miles away from Lisieux. Leonie and Celine moved to temporary quarters near him. They exchanged letters with their sisters.

When Louis disappeared, Therese strove to be brave. She even told another nun that she could bear to suffer more. Not any longer. She felt that her cup of pain overflowed. Therese later referred to these days as "bitter sufferings" (SS 154).

Besides the humiliation of having their father in an institution for the insane and their grief over his suffering, the sisters bore a further trial. Local gossips accused them of causing their father's collapse. Hadn't they abandoned him to enter religious life? Was it coincidence that his first major attack closely followed Marie's profession, and the next Therese's clothing?

Louis was humble and submissive in his confinement. He remained at Bon Sauveur three years. Then on May 12, 1892, Isidore brought him to visit his Carmelite daughters. He looked shriveled and ill to those who had not seen him for so long. He was lucid, but could not speak until the very end of the visit. Then he lifted one finger and said, "To heaven." The nuns would never see him again. He died two years later.

Sorrow and acceptance

This chapter focuses on overcoming our sadness and fears through trust in God. We will learn how early biographies of Therese misrepresented her struggles with these passions. We'll consider the so-called stages of grief. I'll share how my unresolved mistrust caused me to fear for my children's future, and the books that helped me begin to move forward. We'll see how Therese reacted when her greatest childhood fear was realized. And we'll explore how Christ conquered the fear of annihilation, which lies at the root of all other fears.

I love reading about the saints. But sometimes we misinterpret God's will for our lives after reading about theirs. A false reading of a saint's life or teaching can set us up for trouble. Sentimentalized biographies can give us an unrealistic, overly spiritualized view of suffering.

In the first decades after Therese's death, syrupy depictions of her life were common. The Carmelite nuns actually touched up some photos of Therese to make them fit the misleading stories about her. They wanted to depict her as always smiling. They did Therese and all of us an injustice. When we gloss over the trials of the saints or paste a cardboard smile on their faces, we make them something other than human. We can then easily dismiss them and their message as irrelevant.

For decades now, biographers have tried to set the story of Therese straight. But the original syrupy versions of her life have not completely disappeared. They repel many educated and self-described sophisticated people who could have learned from her simplicity.

Saints are human, superbly human. They live life as God intends us all to live it. They suffer as much as we would in their situations. They struggle against sin. They respond to their trials with heroic virtue.

We should not confuse acceptance of grief with denial of it. Just as I used to think that Christians should never get angry at all, I also believed that sorrow meant a lack of trust in God. I thought acceptance of suffering meant not crying, not feeling wounded or lonely or lost. I'm astonished when I recall how recently I realized this was wrong. And it wasn't even my own insight, but a talk with Dan and my brother the monk that opened my eyes.

If a stranger walked into a party and we pretended he wasn't there, would that be acceptance of him? Of course not! It would be rejection. Pretending our grief doesn't exist won't make us holy. That is not trust. It's a refusal to be vulnerable—the very opposite of trust.

We must beware of the opposite error too—giving in to sorrow, indulging it. We must strive to come to a place of acceptance.

We have probably all heard of the so-called five stages of grief: denial, anger, bargaining, depression, and acceptance. Based on the writings of Swiss-born psychologist Elisabeth Kübler-Ross, the five stages are taught in most grief counseling sessions and in college psychology courses. But Kübler-Ross herself has said that her work was misinterpreted. She never intended to teach that everyone must go through five stages of grief in a certain order. Rather, her work detailed common ways her terminally ill patients and their families dealt with grief.

Each of us experiences grief in a unique way. We should never feel guilty for not measuring up to our notion of how a saint would handle grief. Nor should we assume that the expressions of grief we see in others tell the whole story.

Immediately after my sister Terri's death, God gave my parents the grace to accept it. I remember the funeral and reception at our home as a time of quiet acceptance and even joy among the tears. Many friends and relatives were moved by Mom and Dad's attitude. The Holy Spirit worked powerfully in their lives. They were excited about following God whole heartedly. They praised him at once, in the midst of their suffering. But this does not mean that they never grieved!

As an adult, I have heard my mother counsel an acquaintance who feared losing her infant grandchild. After Terri died, I learned, Mom suffered panic attacks. Sometimes she could barely breathe from the force of the grief weighing upon her. She overcame these attacks by repeating the name of Jesus over and over. I was ignorant of this aspect of her grief as a child. I only saw my parents' strength.

Now, forty years after our car accident, I am not ashamed to shed a few tears when Mom and I talk about it. Neither is she. We will feel the loss of Terri until we see her again in heaven. Grief does not completely go away before then. But we have found peace.

Fears for my loved ones

Peace about my future has been harder to come by than peace about my past. For much of my life, I had a hopeful disposition, even though my temperament tends towards seriousness. I encouraged a friend on the brink of despair because of problems in her irregular marriage. I talked another friend through the temptation to suicide. I believed firmly in God's goodness. But as I grew older, that outlook began to change.

The older I got, the more tragedy I observed in the lives of those around me. My nephew contracted leukemia. A friend's daughter died at age four. One of Dan's friends from high school passed away. Life was suddenly fragile. It seemed only a matter of time before sorrow hit me more directly.

At the same time, I was encountering more sin and weakness in my-self than I had realized were there. Striving to follow the teachings of the Carmelite saints, I expected that soon I would have a conversion like

Therese did. I expected God to come and take over the work that I was unable to do. Instead, I saw little progress against sin in my life. I couldn't understand why God would not relieve me of my anger problem, for example.

Getting stuck in the spiritual life caused me to ask questions I would never have considered before. Had the Carmelite saints erred? Was holiness just for the few, not the many? Could I really trust God? Could I even be sure that he existed?

While I was struggling with these questions, an acquaintance of ours whom I'll call Steve, a husband with three small children, took his life. I was not close to the family, although his wife Melissa (not her real name) and their kids were part of our moms' group that met weekly. Yet his death troubled me deeply. He had recently been diagnosed with a mental illness and was desperately trying to get help.

I had just finished reading *I Believe in Love: a Personal Retreat Based on the Teaching of St. Therese of Lisieux* by Fr. Jean d'Elbée. I was recommending it to anyone who would listen. Now, desiring to do something for the grieving widow, I brought my copy to the wake. Dan had already gone to the funeral home and returned to take care of the kids. Now it was my turn to visit and pray.

The funeral home was busy, but not overflowing. I picked up a prayer card from a basket in the entryway before moving on into the inner room. Melissa sat in a chair half way between the door and the open casket at the front. As I stood in line to speak with her, she impressed me with the way she openly shed tears, yet seemed at peace in her soul. I handed her the book, apologizing that it was used. I urged her to trust God with her sorrows.

Then I squeezed her hand and moved on to view the body. When I saw that the couple's little girls had written final letters to their dad to be buried with him, sadness overcame me.

The family could surely use my prayers. But I was the one who was struggling with despair. Why doesn't God protect the weak? Had he ignored all the prayers that Steve and his family had prayed?

How could the survivors endure their loss? I could hardly imagine a greater pain than knowing you hadn't been able to prevent a family member's suicide. I felt like the Devil had triumphed over Steve, despite his Catholic faith. That scared me. *Who of us*, I thought, *is safe? Does God sometimes fail?*

For months I battled these feelings every time I thought of Steve and his family. *Why, God? How? I don't understand*, I prayed dozens of times. Gradually I thought about it less often, but I was not at peace. My doubts gnawed at me.

When political losses in our state and nation marked the advance of the Culture of Death, I asked similar questions. How could my children grow up in the new world that was coming into being? Would they stay faithful to God and the Church? I foresaw suffering and persecution for them if they remained strong, and worse tragedies if they did not. *Why was God allowing these things to happen?*

Several years later—only in 2013, in fact—a reader of my blog asked me to review her book, *Diary of a Country Mother*. Cindy Montanaro wrote a journal covering the year after her young son Tim lost his battle with mental illness. Once again, I felt vulnerable. How could I trust God to watch over us? Why should he protect the Rossini family, when so many others have suffered?

I couldn't understand the peace with which Cindy wrote. Her worst nightmare, the thing she had worked and prayed for years to be spared, had come to pass. How could she bear it without bitterness?

But I had promised to write a review. That meant I had to process what I had read and share it with my readers. In that processing, God began to enlighten me. I realized that the Devil did not have the final word in Tim Montanaro's life. The *Diary* itself spoke a further word, through which God used the boy's suffering to enlighten me.

God has the final word—and that word has not yet been written, even for those who have already died. The final battle of the ages remains to be fought. And in eternity, God can more than make up for the temporal suffering that we endure.

Towards the end of her life, Therese told her companions, "Everything is grace" (LC 57). I chose to believe her rather than my fears. I surrendered the future to God.

Focusing on the present

Worrying about the future is pointless. We can only live in the present. Jesus told his disciples, "Therefore do not be anxious about tomorrow, for tomorrow will be anxious for itself. Let the day's own trouble be sufficient for the day" (Mt 6:34).

God's grace exists in the present. Remember when we discussed the question *what if?* Asking *what if?* distracts us from God's plan. In a similar way, obsessing over the future paralyzes us. It restrains us from doing God's will today. Today we have work to do. We have children to care for, jobs to carry out, prayers to offer. Today we can bring light to a neighbor in darkness. Today we can repent and forgive.

God offers us the grace to endure at the moment that we meet with hardship, not before. A story from the life of Corrie Ten Boom illustrates this wonderfully. Corrie and her family hid Jews from the Nazis during World War II in their home in the Netherlands. Her book *The Hiding Place* tells the story. It also contains significant memories from her childhood. Corrie recalls visiting a family who had just lost a baby with her mother and sister.

She had never witnessed the effects of death before. Death frightened her. She could not eat the rest of the day or sleep that night. Finally, her sister told their father what the matter was. Corrie was terrified that she would someday lose her loved ones, especially her father, whom she particularly loved. She writes:

> Father sat down on the edge of my narrow bed.
>
> "Corrie," he began gently, "when you and I go to Amsterdam—when do I give you your ticket?"
>
> I sniffed a few times, considering this. "Why, just before we get on the train."
>
> "Exactly. And our wise Father in heaven knows when we're going to need things, too. Don't run out ahead of Him, Corrie. When the time comes that some of us will have to die, you will look into your heart and find the strength you need—just in time." (Ada, MI: Chosen Books, 2006, 44)

Corrie's life proved these words true. Her father and sister later died in concentration camps, as did many of their other friends and relatives. Corrie escaped death at Ravensbruck women's prison through a clerical error that she considered a miracle. She endured dark periods, but in the end she surrendered fully to God. She even forgave the prison guards that had abused her and her sister Betsy. If she had known beforehand what she would have to suffer, she could have despaired. But when the time came to suffer, grace to endure that suffering came with it.

The death of Louis Martin

Louis Martin eventually deteriorated enough that the Guerins thought it best for him to live with them. An attack on May 27, 1894, paralyzed one arm. A priest gave him the Anointing of the Sick. Then, on June 5, he had a heart attack. Even so, the Guerins chose not to cancel their annual trip to the seaside at La Musse in July. They took Louis and Celine Martin with them. Leonie, with Therese's encouragement, had entered the Visitation convent once more. Louis passed away peacefully at La Musse on July 29 with Celine at his side.

Now at last Celine would be free to join her sisters in Carmel. She entered on September 14, after debates among the nuns as to the wisdom of accepting another Martin sister. She took the name Sr. Genevieve of the Holy Face.

Therese did not waste the years of her father's illness. She wrote to Celine in 1890, "Now we no longer have anything to hope for on earth . . . nothing is left to us but to suffer" (HF 181). When we come to such a place in life, we have two options: despair or giving ourselves completely to God. Therese chose the second option. "Jesus wants me as an orphan," she wrote. He wanted her to cling only to himself. That could not happen until he tore her from her father. She had been willing to leave Louis behind and be content with parlor visits, but God asked a greater sacrifice.

Therese later wrote that the years of Louis' suffering produced great spiritual growth for every member of the family. She considered those years more beneficial than supernatural ecstasy, and she blessed God for them.

After Louis died, she wrote separately to Celine and Leonie, saying that their father's illness had seemed like a five-year-long death. His ultimate death, which had once been her greatest fear, brought relief. At last God had freed him from pain and humiliation.

Therese had been separated from her father for years. Now she felt him beside her again in spirit. From heaven he watched over his little Queen. She believed that in eternity God would restore the time with her father that he now took from her. The joy of reunion lay ahead (ibid.).

She was not afraid to be weak, even in her sorrow. She saw no shame in admitting that she was grieving and suffering. "Therese reread what Father Pichon had taught during the retreat [before Marie's profession] in 1887. To suffer according to the heart of God, one need not suffer with courage like a hero. It is enough to suffer as Jesus did at Gethsemane" (TL 148).

Fearing death and annihilation

Fr. Groeschel notes that "the fear of eternal loss is universal and is not lightly to be dismissed. It is the mostly deeply rooted of fears" (SP 129). We fear death, because we fear annihilation. As Christians we believe in the afterlife, but at times our faith wavers.

Our culture, advanced in medicine and safety standards, has pushed death to the far corners of existence. Death affects our daily lives much less than it did the lives of our ancestors. The Martin family's losses were common for the period.

Our unfamiliarity with death, coupled with the demise of Christian culture, produces some pathetic offspring, metaphorically speaking. We spend thirty dollars for an ounce of wrinkle cream, thinking that if we stay young looking, we can ward off death. We cling to adolescent attitudes and behaviors. If we never grow up, perhaps we can live forever. We promote assisted suicide in the false belief that if we can control the manner of our death we will find peace. Yet peace eludes us.

In the Garden of Eden, God told Adam and Eve they would die if they ate the forbidden fruit. The Devil temporarily convinced them that they would not die. How soon they realized he had lied! They realized they were naked and vulnerable. Nakedness meant exposure, possible sickness, and death. Only God held the remedy for death. Adam and Eve hid from him. They tried to save themselves. They made clothing out of fig leaves to protect and hide themselves. But death came all the same, to them and all their descendants. Jesus became a man so that

> through death he might destroy him who has the power of death, that is, the devil, and deliver all those who through fear of death were subject to lifelong bondage. (Heb 2: 14–15)

Jesus did not pretend it was easy to go to the Cross. He pleaded with God the Father to relieve him of his suffering. But he added, "Not my will, but thine be done" (Lk 22:42). He raised acceptance of suffering and death to a supernatural level. His natural repugnance towards them taught him perfect submission to the Father's will (see Heb 5:7–10). Jesus on the Cross, naked and dead, cures our fear. For we know that he rose again and promised eternal life to those who follow him. Now,

> Who shall separate us from the love of Christ? Shall tribulation, or distress, or persecution, or famine, or nakedness, or peril, or sword? . . .
>
> No, in all these things we are more than conquerors through him who loved us. For I am sure that neither death, nor life, nor angels, nor principalities, nor things present, nor things to come, nor powers, nor height, nor depth, nor anything else in all creation, will be able to separate us from the love of God in Christ Jesus our Lord. (Rom 8:37–40)

Jesus faced the Devil, sin, and death. He calls us to imitate him. "The trust taught by Christ is not based on a denial of the reality of suffering or evil" (SP 130). On the contrary, as Fr. Groeschel states, denying our fears jeopardizes our spiritual growth (ibid.). We cannot run away from suffering, unless we would run away from the Cross. No matter how much we imagine we control our lives, death will come in the end.

Let us relinquish control to God. Let us learn to say along with God the Son, "Father, your will be done." God is a tender Father, who holds our hands as we "walk through the valley of the shadow of death," (Ps 23:4) and who leads us beyond it to eternal life.

Therese's grieving for her father was natural and healing. She did not have to pretend to be strong. She just had to accept the Father's will. She learned to lean on the Fatherhood of God. She entered even more into the way of spiritual childhood.

Questions for Reflection

1. What are my greatest fears?

2. What are my thoughts on grieving? Have I succumbed to the view that sorrow is ungodly in itself?

3. Do I have unresolved grief that I need to deal with?

Practical Suggestions

* Choose a quote to memorize from below one of the chapter headings of this book. Make sure it is one that speaks to your particular anxieties and fears. Repeat it to yourself throughout the day as needed.

* Pope St. John Paul II began his pontificate by proclaiming, "Be not afraid!" Read a short biography of him. Meditate on the many ways he resisted fear: in traveling all over the world, in forgiving his would-be assassin, in confronting communism, in facing sickness, etc. How can you follow his example?

Chapter Ten
Through Deserts and Darkness

For gold is tested in the fire, and acceptable men in the furnace of humiliation.

Sir 2:5

While Louis was slowly dying, spiritual darkness engulfed Therese. She received no consolations during her many spiritual retreats, starting with the one before her clothing. In fact, according to Fr. Bernard Bro, Therese only had two years without tragedy or darkness from the time her mother died until her own death twenty years later (STL 169).

The greatest darkness would come during her final illness, as she awaited death. But shortly after Therese made her general confession to Fr. Pichon, she experienced prolonged dryness in prayer. Jesus was hiding, as she put it (SL 95).

For five days before her scheduled clothing ceremony in January 1889, Therese went on a private retreat as preparation. She spent three or four hours of every day in prayer. Instead of being joyfully attentive as she was used to, she fell asleep. It seemed that Jesus also slept.

As the Rule required silence, a tradition grew up of Carmelite nuns leaving notes for each other when needed. Mother Marie de Gonzague allowed the nuns under her to do more than just pass necessary messages. She let them write entire letters to each other. These letters did not have to be about work or the spiritual life. They became a substitute for conversation. Even when the nuns went on solitary retreats before special days, she allowed them to communicate in this way.

Therese took advantage of this laxity to share her spirituality and struggles with her sisters (but never to write about trivial matters). She wrote several letters to her sisters during her first retreat. They give us entrance to the hermitage where she prayed alone. Her customary joy in prayer had vanished. "The poor little lamb can say nothing to Jesus, and, above all, Jesus says absolutely nothing to it," she wrote to Sr. Marie of the Sacred Heart (LT 75).

Therese strove to use this new-found silence of God to her advantage. She viewed it as an opportunity to let go of everything, even spiritual comforts. In a letter to Sr. Agnes she made her attitude clear:

> If you only knew how much I want to be indifferent to the things of this earth. What do all created beauties mean to me, I would be unhappy possessing them, my heart would be so empty! (LT 74)

And later she wrote,

> He knows well that if He were to give me a shadow of HAPPINESS, I WOULD ATTACH MYSELF TO IT WITH ALL MY ENERGY, ALL THE STRENGTH OF MY HEART, AND THIS SHADOW HE IS REFUSING ME; HE PREFERS LEAVING ME IN DARKNESS TO GIVING ME A FALSE LIGHT WHICH WOULD NOT BE HIMSELF! (LT 76, emphasis in the original)

When she gave evidence before the Church court on the sanctity of her sister, Sr. Genevieve (Celine) stated that Therese chose the Carmelites rather than another order, because she desired to suffer as much as she could. A teacher or one who ministers to the poor or sick sees the fruits of her work daily. As a cloistered nun praying for priests, Therese was denied this comfort. She chose to "devote herself to the most toilsome of all labors, that of overcoming one's own nature" (HF 142). She knew the desert lay ahead of her, as it did for all Carmelites.

During the days following her conversation with Uncle Isidore about entering Carmel, she experienced prolonged darkness for the first time. The reality of it must have shocked her. In all her other sufferings, she ran to Jesus for comfort. Then he seemed to rebuff her advances. She felt one with Joseph and Mary, as they searched three days for the young Jesus before they could find him (HF 223).

The renewal of her spiritual darkness in Carmel could not have surprised her as much. Still she felt alone. Not only her father, but Jesus too hid his face. Unlike the "martyrdom" of her father's illness, this suffering intensified over time. God concealed himself for the remainder of her life.

Therese's letters to her sisters revealed the depth of her sufferings. Even though she lived in close companionship with the other nuns of the convent, no one beyond her blood sisters suspected her inner darkness. Her companions in Carmel echoed Fr. Pichon's mistaken view of her. They too saw her as a child without problems. If anything, they thought she had an easier life than most of them. After all, three birth sisters and a cousin lived behind the grille with her. They didn't know how she consciously distanced herself from her family members as much as charity allowed. Therese hid herself too—from everyone but God.

The Carmelites knew her for her smile and sense of humor. Novice Mistress Sr. Marie of the Angels said of her, "She can make you weep with devotion and just as easily split your sides with laughter during recreations" (PT 239). Therese had always been a mimic. She continued to amuse her sisters and the other nuns in this way after her profession.

Untouched photos of her show serenity, even though a hint of her pain comes through at times to the close observer.

How should we interpret this peacefulness? Can suffering possibly be deep when one's face, words, and actions show little sign of it? People who have never experienced spiritual darkness might think it is easier to bear than other types of suffering. They would be greatly mistaken.

A taste of spiritual darkness

In this chapter we'll discuss the meaning and purpose of dryness in prayer. Then we'll see what the three brave young men from the book of Daniel teach us about God's presence in our suffering. But first I'll share an experience with spiritual darkness from my college years. Most of the names in this story have been changed.

Through much of high school and all my vacations from college I worked full time at a Super Valu grocery store. I attended a Protestant college out of state. Though an ardent Christian, I undervalued my Catholic faith at that time. Poorly catechized, I considered leaving the Catholic Church.

At college I belonged to an ecumenical charismatic prayer group. We met together regularly for prayer and Bible study. We supported one another against the secular culture around us. My friends numbered in the double digits. I spent part of every day with several of them.

In contrast, I had few close friends during my high school years. Returning home for the summer after my sophomore year of college, I left an active social life behind me. I longed for Christian fellowship.

Coming home also presented spiritual challenges. College life gave me independence. I controlled my schedule and made decisions for my daily life. I interacted with peers when I chose, and retired to my dorm room when I needed quiet. I avoided people I struggled to get along with. I was responsible only for myself. Good behavior came relatively easily.

At home, my parents owned the car, set the dinner hour, and established the rules. I had to interact with siblings, whether I wanted to or not, even those whose temperaments clashed with mine. I felt as if noise, arguments, and rebellion constantly swirled around me.

My interior life mirrored the exterior chaos. I argued and complained, and condemned myself for doing so. I thought I was beyond such behavior! I prayed, fasted, and read the Bible to grow in virtue. I resolved to behave better. As I was destined to do in later years, I failed. Why was I so powerless? What was I missing? Desperation to be free from my weakness seized me.

One evening two friendly young women approached my cash register at work. In looks they contrasted one another—one with dark, permed hair, the other with long blonde hair and striking green eyes. They purchased bread and fish. The brunette explained that they were holding a Bible study for young people at their apartment just a few blocks away. They were discussing the feeding of the five thousand.

When I expressed interest, they invited me out for lunch on the weekend at a nearby Perkins. The brunette introduced herself as Renee. The blonde was named Ginny. *God is answering my prayer!* I rejoiced. Fellowship with other Christians my age would pull me out of my loneliness and strengthen me to overcome my faults.

At Perkins on Saturday a third woman joined us. Her name was Sandy. Ginny explained that they had a Bible study for individual reflection they would like to share with me, rather than inviting me to join their Wednesday night group right away. I found that a little unusual, but did not stop to analyze it too much. I was so grateful to find women my age who were striving to serve God more fully!

Sandy was somewhat more reserved than the other two, but they encouraged her to lead our conversations. She asked me various questions about my religious background and beliefs. I eagerly shared some of the charismatic experiences from my prayer group at school. “I don’t know what you think about the baptism in the Holy Spirit,” I said, “but I know it’s from God.” They did not respond to my implied question. This happened several times over the course of our conversation. Sandy asked a question, I answered with my beliefs and hinted that I’d like to know what they thought, but they never spoke candidly. When I asked what church they attended, they told me it was nondenominational. They did not elaborate.

Now this would have troubled any reasonable adult in my place. It frustrated me, but I tried to overlook it. I avoided “rude” questions. For once I was trusting someone *too much.*

Over the next two weeks, the four of us met a handful of times, sometimes at restaurants, sometimes at the apartment that Renee, Ginny, and Sandy shared with one other woman from their church. I recall one session where we discussed Galatians 5:19–21:

> The acts of the sinful nature are obvious: sexual immorality, impurity and debauchery; idolatry and witchcraft; hatred, discord, jealousy, fits of rage, selfish ambition, dissensions, factions and envy; drunkenness, orgies, and the like. I warn you, as I did before, that those who live like this will not inherit the kingdom of God. (NIV)

Sandy leaned on the dining room table and quizzed me after reading this passage aloud. “Have you fallen into sexual immorality? Practiced magic? Felt jealous? Had fits of rage?” I acknowledged my anger problem. I admitted I was sometimes selfish or jealous. Who hasn’t committed at least one of these sins? I did not suspect how my answers would later be used against me.

At last we completed the personal Bible studies. To "celebrate," the girls invited me to a slumber party the following Friday. “My mom and dad are going out of town and I'm house-sitting for them," Ginny said. "They live just a few blocks away. Why don't you all come over and keep me company?"

"I have to work until eleven," I said, disappointed because it sounded like fun.

"No problem," Renee replied. "You can come over here to our apartment afterwards, and we'll go to Ginny's parents' together. Will you have a chance to eat supper?"

"Not much."

"Then we'll order pizza," she said. "We can watch a movie we have about the book of Acts."

On Friday I arrived at their apartment shortly after 11 P.M. To my surprise, Ginny was already there. No one mentioned anything about going to her parents' house. Nor did anyone order pizza or offer me anything to eat or drink. My stomach was already growling, sometimes loud enough for everyone to hear, but I didn't want to be impolite. I resigned myself just to watching a movie and going to bed for the night. That did not happen either.

Instead of watching a video, we sat in the living room to talk. A few minutes later the doorbell rang. My new "friends" introduced me to Laura. Somewhat older than us, Laura had an official role in their church (the name of which I still did not know). "Laura's here to liven things up," Renee said. That too was false. Laura meant to convince me to join their church.

Laura took a seat next to me and began reviewing what I had told the others in our study sessions. Naively I had assumed my words were confidential. Now Laura said that the sins I had confessed to them showed I was not on the road to heaven. Fits of rage? Galatians said that disqualified me. That was just one problem among many. "I used to be a pagan, Connie," Laura said, "but you are a Pharisee. You need to repent so you can be saved."

I opened my mouth, speechless. "I can't accept that," I said at last. "That is absolutely not true."

"Well, that's the teaching of Paul," Laura replied. "The Bible is the Word of God. Let's look at some more Scripture, and you'll see this is the truth."

Back and forth we went like this for hours. I can't remember most of the Bible passages we consulted. Every time I protested, Laura brought another verse from her arsenal.

"God is displeased with you," she said. "If you were to die, you would go to hell." I looked at Renee, Ginny, and Sandy. They nodded their heads in agreement.

Insulted, degraded, wounded, I felt tears pouring down my cheeks. "I just can't accept this right now," I said. "I need some time to think." I expected Laura to stop the attack at these words, but she did not even pause.

"You need to be baptized by immersion," she told me. "Then the Holy Spirit will give you the power to overcome all your sins. You have not been a true Christian. Sin has no power over Christians. They can stop sinning instantly the moment their sins are pointed out. You've told us that you can't overcome some of your sins. That means the Holy Spirit isn't living in you. You are living according to the sinful nature."

"I need some time to think and pray," I said. Still, she gave me no relief.

This religious browbeating lasted most of the night. My mind was spinning. I had read the Bible cover to cover more than once, and memorized the order of the books of the New Testament as a child. But now when Laura directed me to a Bible verse, I could no longer locate the right book. Renee had to find the passages in my Bible for me. More than once, I asked to go home. I was stuck there without a car of my own, completely at the mercy of my hosts. They ignored all my requests.

Finally, like a tortured prisoner who confesses to crimes he has never committed, I agreed to join their church.

Renee offered me a glass of water. Then Laura left. They let me sleep on their couch.

Too early in the morning, Laura was back for more. This time she wanted to tackle the problem of my charismatic spirituality. I refused to budge on that point. At last they drove me home.

That day and the following night were terrible. I had to work the noon-to-eight shift, the most dreaded Saturday schedule. My stomach was in knots. My thoughts raced. At times I rejected the religious views of my "friends" and peace flooded in. I knew I was really a Christian. I knew God had worked in my life. But a few minutes later, I asked myself, *What if they're right?* Then my confusion and anxiety returned. How could I ever be sure? How could I ignore them and walk away without a nagging feeling for the rest of my life that I was outside God's grace?

I tossed and turned most of that night. I told no one else what I was experiencing.

The hardest thing to bear was my supposed separation from God. All my life I had attempted to serve him. Now I was accused of being a Pharisee and a hypocrite who needed to be saved. I prayed aloud in my room, "Lord, if they're right, I don't know who you are." The God I thought I knew would not condemn me for ignorance, when I was well intentioned. Laura claimed that God only hears the prayers of the saved, so I feared he was deaf to my cries. I spoke into a void that did not answer me. I felt completely cut off from the one who had been my closest companion. Darkness encompassed me.

The next day was Sunday. I awoke with serious doubts about what Laura had said. Renee called me early and asked how I was doing. I tried to be balanced and rational. "I think you're partly right, but I think the charismatic movement is right too."

Renee invited me to attend church with them that day. "If you just come to our church, you'll know," she said. "You'll be amazed by all the love you find."

By now I knew that they belonged to the Twin Cities Church of Christ, part of the larger International Churches of Christ. The group, I later learned, had been banned from dozens of college campuses due to its cult-like recruiting methods and authoritarian structure. Its Twin Cities affiliate no longer exists, but was very active in the 1980s and 90s. The denomination as a whole (yes, I will call it a denomination, even though they don't like that designation) has been reformed in the past decade, so some of the problems I experienced may have been corrected.

Other people I know underwent similar deception and manipulation. A friend's sister later joined one of their churches in New York. She also claimed her Catholic family was "unsaved." An acquaintance of mine, against my advice, attended a Twin Cities Church of Christ service after finding a flyer on her car's windshield. When she asked them about my experience, they expressed surprise and indignation. One woman accused me of making it up. She was a blond with beautiful green eyes who had introduced herself as Ginny.

That Sunday in 1988, my parents reluctantly agreed to let me attend church with Renee and the others that morning. I rode with Renee, Ginny, and Sandy. In his sermon, the pastor repeated what Laura had said on Friday night. Many other visitors were in a similar situation to mine. This Sunday marked the end of a week of concerted "evangelization" efforts. Everything in the service was aimed at reinforcing the message we had been given. I and many others went forward for the "altar call" (there was, of course, no altar—in fact, the service was held in a school gym with no semblance of a church about it). Tears streamed down my face again.

Love had not convinced me. I had known genuine Christian love all my life. Instead, my vulnerable state, the repetition of fearful doctrine, and the number of people who opposed me determined my decision. I was afraid of being rejected by God and sought an end to my anguish.

The next step was to be baptized. But before that, we had to "count the cost." We met as a small group again, in the park surrounding Lake Nikomis, just a few blocks from my home. Renee told me that my parents would say I was involved in a cult. She tried to persuade me to be baptized before I spoke to them, but I could not do that. I owed my parents more respect. Then Renee and the others told me how their loved ones had tried to dissuade them from their beliefs. "What will you say if your parents ask why you can't keep going to their church? What if they say you don't need to be baptized again? What if they say you've been brainwashed?"

They raised every foreseeable objection and made me rehearse my answers. When at last my responses satisfied them, they drove me home. They waited outside in the car, while I went in to talk to Mom and Dad.

Poor Mom tried to help me mostly on her own, because Dad was too laid back to stand in the way of anything I wanted to do. She knew right away that I had been brainwashed. But of course I rolled my eyes at that suggestion. I had expected it. *Mom is always blowing things out of proportion,* I thought.

"I don't want you to see or speak to those girls for thirty days," she said. "If you still feel the same way then, you can join their church."

"I can't do that," I said. She had no idea of what I had suffered the last two days. I didn't think I could survive a month like that! Besides, what if I changed my mind in that time? What if I lost my chance of salvation?

Finally, when Mom realized that my "friends" were waiting for me out in the car, she decided to act. She would tell them herself that they could not contact me for thirty days. I tried to brush past her and run outside. "Grab her, Jack," she said to Dad. "Hold her while I go out and tell them to leave."

So Dad held me tightly by the arms while Mom went out to talk to them. I knew better than to struggle against Dad. I could never win.

After the car pulled away, darkness and confusion overwhelmed me again. I fought against it like a drowning man fights for air.

On Monday evening after work, I went to visit Naomi, the mother of my best friend from high school. She was a Pentecostal. I wanted to know what her church taught about Baptism and salvation. When I told her Laura and the others had said I was not a Christian, Naomi laughed. Laughed! Laughter was the one thing I was not prepared to face. No one had coached me on a rebuttal for it, as they had coached me to rebut so many other reactions to my decision. Naomi's laughter broke through my mental fog and helped me to see the truth. I owe this non-Catholic woman my return to sanity and the true Church.

Years later I shared this entire story with a friend of mine. In the midst of a completely different type of trial herself, she could not understand the depth of this spiritual darkness. After all, it had only lasted a few days. But when these self-appointed disciples took Jesus from me, they took everything. They left me destitute.

During those days of confusion, I never could have joked with others, looked serene, or sincerely smiled. Therese not only did these things, she had a deep peace in the center of her soul even as darkness flooded the rest of her being. I only wish I had trusted God as she did.

Why is prayer sometimes dry?

Spiritual darkness takes many forms. I remember a friend in college lamenting once that she had lost the joy she used to experience in prayer. As a non-Catholic Christian, she believed she must have some hidden sin that kept God distant. Although a poorly formed Catholic at that time myself, I had learned somewhere that dryness in prayer is not necessarily bad. Dryness or aridity in prayer can have many causes. Sometimes it signals spiritual growth.

My college friend's assumption was only partially wrong. Sin can cause prayer to feel uncomfortable. When we feel distant from God, the obvious first thing to consider is whether we are. Have we committed serious sin? Have we been lax about avoiding venial sins? Is it months since we went to the Sacrament of Reconciliation?

We don't want to become scrupulous. If we sincerely try to follow God, he will show us our faults in his time. If we suspect something is wrong with our relationship with him but can't pinpoint the problem, we may need to consult a priest, spiritual director, or wise friend.

Dryness in prayer can also come from the normal ups and downs of our emotions. Just as we do not always feel the love we have for our spouses, kids, or other important people in our lives, we won't always feel our love for God. Love can exist without feelings.

Our health also affects our prayer. Sickness, stress, or depression can make prayer feel empty. But we never waste our time when we pray sincerely. God is still there.

Some days parenting so exhausts me that I can barely think when I sit down to pray. I can barely feel. I can only sit in silence and allow God to pour his love on me for the length of my prayer time.

Finally, dryness in prayer sometimes indicates that God wants to lead us into a closer relationship with him. During our spiritual infancy, God treats us like a mother treats her baby. He holds us close. He smoothes our way. New converts or those recommitting themselves to Christ overflow with joy. God pours his love on them in an almost tangible way. But infancy should not last a lifetime. God might make prayer harder, in order to strengthen our love for him.

We may experience dryness in prayer at any spot along the road to God. Nearly everybody journeys through certain deserts. During the transitions between the major stages in the spiritual life, the scorching winds of God's love purge us from our reliance on anything but him.

God used dry, empty prayer to detach Therese from spiritual consolations.

St. John of the Cross calls these dry stretches of the spiritual life that God initiates, "dark nights." The dark nights might be short. They might last for years. Some people experience them off and on again over decades, with the dark periods growing in frequency and duration.

The dark nights present a special opportunity to grow in trust. Remember playing Blind Man's Bluff as a child? Players pair up. One ties a scarf over his eyes. The other directs him by words or with his hands. The "blind" participant must trust that his friend won't lead him into danger. He is almost totally helpless to protect himself.

The dark nights work in a similar way. Blind to God's action in our lives, or the least sign of his presence, we learn to trust that he is still there, directing our path. We release complete control of our spiritual lives to him, because only he can see the path before us.

This type of dryness in prayer signals the need for a spiritual director, if we do not already have one. We may have to fight to maintain a peaceful attitude. But peace and freedom will result from the dark nights if we use them properly.

My spiritual darkness was not properly what St. John of the Cross calls the Dark Night of the Soul, because natural circumstances produced it, rather than God's secret work. But on a psychological level the pain I experienced was of the same general type.

My interaction with the members of the Twin Cities Church of Christ made me more suspicious of other people's motives. For a long time afterwards, I also cringed at the thought of Purgatory. I felt I had already experienced it. I begged God not to make me go through such pain again.

The fiery furnace

The book of Daniel tells the well-known story of the three brave young men. We remember them by their Babylonian names: Shadrach, Meshach, and Abednego. The Babylonians had captured Jerusalem and taken many of the people of Judah into exile. King Nebuchadnezzar constructed an idol of himself in his capital. He ordered the people to bow down to it whenever his musicians sounded certain notes. Shadrach, Meshach, and Abednego refused to obey. So Nebuchadnezzar sentenced them to death in a blazing hot furnace. Hearing the sentence, they said to the king,

> Our God whom we serve is able to deliver us from the burning fiery furnace; and he will deliver us out of your hand, O king. But if not, be it known to you, O king, that we will not serve your gods or worship the golden image which you have set up. (Dn 3:17–18)

They believed ahead of time that God would miraculously rescue them, but committed to doing his will, even if he did not rescue them, even if he left them to face an excruciating death.

Guards bound the men hand and foot. They heated the furnace so high that those who threw the three men in died from the heat. But Shadrach, Meshach, and Abednego were unscathed. The angel of the Lord—probably the Second Person of the Trinity himself—appeared in the furnace with them. Together, the four of them walked around in the flames, praising God.

This story teaches an obvious lesson. When we undergo terrible suffering, God accompanies us, even when we can't see him, hear him, or feel him. He draws especially near to those who feel abandoned by him, for Jesus himself felt abandoned by the Father on the Cross. The Father did not, could not, abandon his Son. He did not abandon Shadrach, Meshach, and Abednego. He was with Therese in her spiritual darkness. He was with me in mine.

Jesus said, "And remember, I am with you always, to the end of the age" (Mt 28:20). We can rely on those words, no matter what comes. Even if we are too heartsick to sing like the three young men, or make jokes as Therese did, we can still have interior peace.

As she neared death, Therese meditated on this story of the three young men. She said, "If I go to Purgatory, I'll be very content, I'll do like the three Hebrews in the furnace, I'll walk around in the flames singing the canticle of Love" (LC 81).

"I don't know whether I'll go to purgatory or not," she said at another time, "but I'm not in the least bit disturbed about it" (LC 56). She readily accepted anything that came from the hand of God.

I still would rather go straight to heaven than spend time in Purgatory. Who wouldn't? But Therese has taught me that we can endure everything when we trust God. I no longer fear spiritual darkness or temporal punishment for my sins. I look forward to the purification I will face either in this life or afterwards—not because I enjoy suffering, but because each moment of purification will bring me one moment closer to seeing God's face.

Questions for Reflection

1. Have I ever felt abandoned by God? Looking back, can I now see signs of his presence with me?

2. Is my prayer full of consolations, arid, or somewhere in between?

Practical Suggestions

* If you are experiencing prolonged dryness in prayer without understanding the reason, consult a spiritual director or priest. Start by calling your parish. If your pastor or associate is unable to help you, he may be able to direct you to someone who can. Fr. Thomas Dubay's *Fire Within* also gives practical help for discerning whether you are experiencing one of the supernatural dark nights in prayer.

* The Psalms provide wonderful prayers we can pray when our hearts are too heavy to express themselves. Jesus quoted Psalm 22 on the Cross. It begins with the words, "My God, my God, why hast thou forsaken me?" Psalm 37 speaks of triumphing over one's enemies. Psalm 40 urges us to trust God in the midst of suffering. Psalm 116 is the prayer of a man thankful for deliverance from suffering. Commit some of these passages to heart for future support in times of darkness.

Chapter Eleven
Accepting Ourselves and Our Daily Circumstances

I have been crucified with Christ; it is no longer I who live, but Christ who lives in me.

Gal 2:20

On February 20, 1893, the nuns of the Lisieux Carmel elected Sr. Agnes as prioress. The woman who had acted as Therese's mother for so many years of her childhood became her mother in religious life. As one of her first official acts, she appointed Mother Marie de Gonzague as novice mistress. This was the custom for former prioresses. Mother Agnes also appointed Therese as Mother Marie's assistant. For the next few years, Therese effectively ran the novitiate without the title.

Therese directed two novices at first. Shy and reserved Sr. Marie-Madeleine often skipped her required daily meeting with Therese. According to her death notice, she endured unspecified trauma while living as a domestic servant as a young teen. She feared intimacy. Therese bore with her patiently and lovingly. She even wrote a poem about Marie-Madeleine, calling her a queen, who would reign close to Jesus while still on earth (*The Poetry of St. Therese of Lisieux: Complete Edition*, Washington, DC: ICS Publications, 2013). Therese believed trust in Jesus would conquer her fears.

After Therese's death, Marie-Madeleine suddenly blossomed, amazing herself with her profound trust in God.

Sr. Marie of the Trinity, the second novice, also benefitted from Therese's wisdom. After private counseling with Therese, she tore herself away from improper attachment to Mother Marie de Gonzague.

About the same time that Therese took over the novitiate, Mother Agnes removed her from working in the sacristy and made her assistant to the portress. The nuns' gate-keeper, a kindly but eccentric nun, refined Therese's charity while growing in appreciation for her discretion. Mother Agnes also appointed Therese to paint devotional pictures and write religious poetry for the community.

That summer, Therese painted a fresco of angels in the invalids' oratory. In the fresco, twelve little cherubs surround the golden doors of the tabernacle that is built into the wall. Three children accompany them. One holds an incense burner, symbolizing our prayers rising to heaven. One holds grapes and wheat, symbolizing the Eucharist. The third holds a harp and sleeps, leaning on the tabernacle. This child represents Therese herself.

Therese often fell asleep during mental prayer. She writes:

> I should be desolate for having slept (for seven years) during my hours of prayer and my thanksgivings after Holy Communion; well, I am not desolate. I remember that little children are pleasing to their parents when they are asleep as well as when they are wide awake; I remember, too, that when they perform operations, doctors put their patients to sleep. Finally, I remember that: "The Lord knows our weakness, that he is mindful that we are but dust and ashes." (SS 165)

When Therese says, *I should,* she refers to popular opinion about sanctity. The moral rigidity of French Catholic culture expected everyone to be strong. Therese was not.

Therese understood human nature. She was a realist, both with herself and with others. She did not expect extraordinary strength, wisdom, or goodness. We don't expect great things of little children.

On the other hand, she scolded her charges for their lack of confidence in God. She pointed out their smallest faults and showed them the remedies. She required them to seek holiness, but not through their strength. Only surrender to God would sanctify them.

Besides her relatives and the novices under her, the sisters in the convent knew little about Therese's mature spiritual life. They saw her removed from physical duties so that she did not even have to help with the laundry any more. Some believed that Mother Agnes pampered her, that she brought no benefit to the community at large. Some even questioned if she had entered Carmel just to "amuse herself" (SL 129).

But the novices saw more clearly. As "senior novice" as she was now called, Therese developed the gifts needed for spiritual direction. Her wisdom and maturity shone in this new position. Gorres points out that, although Therese followed the little way herself, she did not try to remake her charges in her image. Instead, she noted the qualities and temperament of each sister and adapted her spiritual direction to fit them.

> I saw from the very beginning that everyone has to go through much the same struggle, though from another point of view there are vast differences between one soul and another; and because they are so different, I can never treat them in the same way. (HF 322)

Sr. Marie of the Trinity was a temperamental novice, who, like Therese in former years, cried often. One day, Therese stood at her easel, carefully painting a gold vine around a portrait of the child Jesus appearing to St. Teresa. She planned to give the painting to Celine for her twenty-fifth birthday. Marie of the Trinity approached, her large, deep-set eyes rimmed in tears. Therese had tried all the usual methods to help this sister overcome her lack of self-control, but neither penances nor resolutions nor reprimands worked.

"Tears again, sister?" she asked. "We must cure you of that." Therese paused, looking to the child Jesus for help. Her eyes swept the room. "I know!" On an inspiration, she picked up a shell from her painting table. "Here," she said, holding it under one of her companion's eyes. "Your tears are too precious to let them fall in such a wasteful manner. I will collect them in this shell."

Marie of the Trinity raised her hands to protest, but Therese gently grabbed them with her free hand. "No wiping now," Therese said. "I don't want to miss a drop." Marie of the Trinity laughed.

"That's better," said Therese. "I believe I got them all." She pressed the shell into Marie's hand. "I want you to keep this. Every time you start to cry, collect your tears in the shell. You may cry as much as you like, as long as you collect every tear. When the shell is full—that's it. No more tears for that day."

Therese's humor worked where nothing else had. From that day, Marie of the Trinity began gaining control over her emotions. She had to move the shell so quickly from eyelid to eyelid in order not to miss any tears, that she couldn't think about what had saddened her. Her tears dried up.

Later, when Therese was on her deathbed, she noticed that Marie of the Trinity had been crying at the thought of losing her. "Have you been using your shell?" Therese asked.

Marie of the Trinity shook her head.

"You must promise me you will use it faithfully after I die. It is of the first importance for your soul."

Marie promised, but also asked permission to be allowed to cry more copiously at Therese's death.

"I will allow you to cry more for the first few days," said Therese, "because I pity your weakness. But after that, you must go back to using the shell." (See NPPO of Sr. Marie of the Trinity.)

Seeing ourselves as God sees us

"There are far more differences between souls than there are between faces," Therese wrote (TL 248). This chapter discusses the differences in our natural strengths and weaknesses. We will learn that God calls everyone to a deep relationship with him. We will see why comparing ourselves with others is dangerous. Finally, we'll learn about an unusual request Therese made, in keeping with her little way.

When we study photographs of the nuns of the Carmel at Lisieux, the first thing we see is the nuns' similarity. We notice the novices, distinguished by their white veils. The remaining nuns hide their individual personalities until we peer more closely. Under the dark veils and white caps, a variety of faces gaze back at us. Some are wrinkled, others fresh with youth. One looks annoyed, another thoughtful. Mother Marie de Gonzague has serious eyes, but a happy mouth. We see the family resemblance in the faces of the Martin sisters. But beyond that, Mother Agnes' face is long and shows the cares of her office. Sr. Marie's is round and plain. Sr. Genevieve's is open. And Therese has her pointed chin and look of quiet contentment.

Behind each of these faces dwells a unique soul, created by God for eternal intimacy with him. God designed a distinctive plan for each of them and for each of us.

Do we see other Christians as our brothers and sisters, or as our rivals in grace? Does praise for others discourage us?

When a novice expressed her envy that she did not possess the same social graces as some of the nuns, Therese reprimanded her.

> Whenever you feel this temptation, pray as follows: "My God, I rejoice that I have no fine and delicate feelings, and I rejoice to find them in others." That will be more pleasing to God than if you were always irreproachable. (HF 330)

Another time, Therese advised Sr. Genevieve that her wish to memorize Scripture as well as Therese was folly and a distraction. She must not build her confidence on natural talents (ibid.).

God has loved each of us since the beginning of time.

> He chose us in him before the foundation of the world, that we should be holy and blameless before him. He destined us in love to be his sons through Jesus Christ, according to the purpose of his will. (Eph 1:4–5)

He gave each of us natural human talents and virtues, and allowed our natural defects. Sin tempts each in different ways. We may struggle with some of the same sins, but not in exactly the same manner. We also each have characteristics that may be an advantage or a disadvantage, depending on the situation.

At the beginning of my existence, God breathed life into me, creating my unrepeatable soul. My soul bears the wounds of Original Sin, but retains a natural goodness. I was made in God's image and likeness, just as Adam and Eve were. Not only my parents, but God himself performed an act of love to bring me into being.

In trusting God, I need to trust that he foresaw my gifts and my defects. He incorporated them into his plan for my life. I need to accept my limitations—not just my spiritual limitations, but also my physical, mental, and psychological limitations. I must accept the challenges of my temperament.

God can use us and accomplish his work in our lives today. He can use our assets and our defects to bring us and those around us closer to him. We should not be overly concerned with personality traits—although understanding them can help us understand God's will for our lives. Centering too much on them can focus our sight on ourselves, rather than raising it to God.

As a child, Therese did not idle her spiritual life while she tried to overcome her sensitivity. By the time God himself relieved her of this flaw, holiness lay within her reach. Often personality problems disappear as a soul grows in intimacy with Christ. Those that remain can remind us of our poverty and weakness before God.

We can be saints too

Therese wrote further about the differences in souls:

> God willed to create great souls comparable to Lilies and Roses, but He has created smaller ones and these must be content to be daisies or violets destined to give joy to God's glances when He looks down at his feet. Perfection consists in doing His will, in being what He wills us to be. (SS 14, punctuation in the original)

When we purchased our first home in La Crosse, we acquired a magazine-worthy flower garden. The former owner had cultivated it for over twenty years, the last few while in retirement. I searched the Internet, seed catalogs, and my new gardening encyclopedia in order to learn the names and requirements of the different flowers. Narcissus, tiger lilies, Russian sage, and brown-eyed Susans took their turns blooming amid hostas and daylilies. Besides having its own bloom time and duration, each species needed to be deadheaded or pruned in its own way. Some called for extra water. Some needed to be staked or protected from pests. Others thrived when left alone.

I had always preferred autumn among the seasons. By our second long winter in Wisconsin, I watched eagerly for the first hint of green to poke through the soil. I knew what would follow. Over the course of the next six months, every shade of blue and red would grace our backyard, along with oranges, yellows, and pure white. Some flowers, like the orange poppies, bloomed spectacularly for just a few days. Others, like the perennial geraniums, bloomed over many weeks, then left neat mounds of green when their blooms were through. The bee balm spiced the air, the roses sweetened it.

I started each spring working diligently among the plants, tending to each with love. But by the time summer reached its height, the garden had gotten ahead of me. There were too many plants for me to keep up with, when I also had to keep up with three little boys.

God, on the other hand, tends to the plants in his garden faithfully, giving each the care it needs. He is neither hurried nor anxious. He is patient and persevering. He knows what each plant requires. He delights in the variety of his garden.

Should a violet envy lilies? Should a daisy envy roses?

Spiritual envy tempts us towards despair. We read about the graces God gave Therese and think, *That's not fair. Why didn't he give such graces to me? I'd like to be a saint too.*

Many Catholic theologians teach that God loves some souls more than others. Otherwise, they argue, everyone would be equal in holiness. This notion has always bothered me. I suspect my discomfort is partly secret discomfort with myself. I do not want to accept my limitations. I want to believe that I am as strong, as intelligent, and as talented (let alone as holy) as the next person. In reality, each of us is irreplaceable, different as to gifts, but of the same immense value, made in God's image.

Questions about God's separate plans for each of us should not bother me too much. Should I impose my limited, human notion of fairness on God? Do I expect to understand all his ways? Or do I trust him enough to believe that his way is good and right, even if I cannot understand it?

We will probably never know on earth how much God predetermines our ultimate level of holiness, and how much depends on our free choice. And it doesn't matter.

Does God divide the world in two—saints and the rest of us? This is the question that should concern us. Therese answers a firm *no.* According to her teaching, God created every soul in his garden to be a saint. Some are greater, some are lesser.

The Second Vatican Council agrees:

> Fortified by so many and such powerful means of salvation, all the faithful, whatever their condition or state, are called by the Lord, each in his own way, to that perfect holiness whereby the Father Himself is perfect. (*Lumen Gentium* 11)

God gave each of us enough to become holy. If he gave certain souls extra help beyond that, why should it concern us? He made each of us just as he desires, and that should suffice. Since he is all good, all powerful, all loving, all just, I must defer to him. I must embrace my weaknesses, in so far as I cannot change them.

St. Paul wrote:

> If the whole body were an eye, where would be the hearing? If the whole body were an ear, where would be the

> sense of smell? But as it is, God arranged the organs in the body, each one of them, as he chose. If all were a single organ, where would the body be? As it is, there are many parts, yet one body. The eye cannot say to the hand, 'I have no need of you,' nor again the head to the feet, 'I have no need of you.' On the contrary, the parts of the body which seem to be weaker are indispensable. (1 Cor 12:17–22)

Even if we are weak, we are indispensable to God's plan for the Church!

God made us to be a saints, whether we are laid back or aggressive, spontaneous or practical; whether we make friends easily, or find ourselves often alone; whether everyone or no one listens to us; whether we succeed in life or apparently fail; whether he calls us to be priests, religious, married, or single; whether we are old or young; whether we are healthy or bedridden; without regard to our physical appearance.

The Lord knows what each of us needs in order to be holy. He directs our paths, tailoring our circumstances and the graces he offers us to our individual souls, which he knows so intimately. Any soul who yields to God's grace can be a vessel of his love (HF 341).

It's not fair

Kathy (not her real name) was a college friend of mine and a recovering alcoholic. She grew up in rural Wyoming, where her parents owned a bar. She and her sister learned to drink and play pool at an early age. Both had drinking problems as adults. After giving their lives to Christ, they fought to remain sober.

When Kathy experienced stress or marked a birthday, the temptation to drink was especially strong. Sometimes other friends and I toured around Sioux Falls, South Dakota in the evenings, searching for her car in the parking lots of the city's bars. Whenever we didn't hear from her for a few days, we got worried. Was she hiding somewhere on a binge?

One spring during our friendship, I felt God was calling me to give up recreational reading for a month. For the average person, this involves no sacrifice at all. But I have always read every chance I could. I used to joke that my tombstone would read, "She died from an overdose of fiction." I struggled to say *yes* to God. I couldn't imagine life without books for thirty days. At last, I gave in.

When I told Kathy about my struggle, she stared at me in disbelief. "It's not fair," she said. "I have to fight against getting drunk, and you're worried about reading too much? You have it so easy!"

I felt guilty. It wasn't easy for me to give up books, but of course I preferred struggling against too much Jane Austen to struggling against too much Jack Daniels. I knew Kathy's life was filled with trials. Besides her early alcoholism, she also bounced around foster homes. One foster father sexually abused her. She didn't know what a stable, Christian family looked like. Though she idealized my upbringing, I agreed wholeheartedly that it was wonderful compared to hers.

I know many people who have had more difficult relationships, endured greater tragedies, and been tempted to more serious sin than I have. I should be a saint by now, with all the advantages God has given me. "Every one to whom much is given, of him will much be required" (Lk 12:48).

A passage from Evelyn Waugh's novel *Brideshead Revisited* that has always troubled me presents an odd paradox on a related topic. Lady Marchmain is trying to convert Charles Ryder to Catholicism. She tells him about her background:

> I became very rich. It used to worry me, and I thought it wrong to possess so many beautiful things when others had nothing. Now I realize that it is possible for the rich

> to sin by coveting the privileges of the poor. The poor have always been the favorites of God and His saints. (Boston: Little, Brown, and Co., 1973, 126–27)

I never understood this passage. I always viewed this as a lame attempt on the part of Lady Marchmain to justify her style of living (or of the author to justify his). Lately I have taken a different view. Now I believe that it is possible for the "righteous" to sin by coveting the "privileges" of penitents. The Gospel clearly favors the poor. It also favors the fallen. Jesus said "I have not come to call the righteous, but sinners to repentance" (Lk 5:32).

Among those who have reached the age of reason, only Jesus and Mary never sinned. They needed no repentance. Nevertheless, some people find it easier to live a moral life than others. Are the upright shut out from salvation? Did Jesus come for others, and not for them?

Absolutely not! For while "sinners" may have to battle lust, the "righteous" have to battle pride. And pride, though traditionally more respectable, is the greater sin.

The Penitent Woman knew she needed grace in order to be good. Simon the Pharisee tried to be good through his own power. Which one should we pity more? The one who finds it easy to place no trust in herself, or the one who doesn't even realize he needs to trust God? Which one has the greatest cause to say, "It's not fair!" Don't both of them have a good argument?

No one gets to heaven without struggling against sin. The little way is still the narrow way. Everyone labors. One is tempted toward presumption, while another is tempted toward despair.

Let us resolve to stop comparing ourselves to our neighbors—either to boast about how much better we are than they, or to envy the ease with which they seem to go through life. Such comparisons are distractions. They distract us from trusting God, who gives us the particular graces we need to grow close to him.

Making acts of faith

After several weeks of practice, I established the habit of asking God for a kiss every time I sinned. The more I practiced it, the more interior peace I enjoyed. My boys were no less noisy, messy, or disobedient than before. Nor did I respond to them much more patiently. But I was much more patient with myself. I knew my day no longer had to spiral out of control because of one angry word. I knew that needn't make the whole day a failure, unless I allowed it to. I knew God was neither shocked by my sin nor disappointed with me.

Then I decided it was time to take trust one step further. Lent provided the opportunity to add another practice to my days. I tried to accept everything that happened during the day as a part of God's plan for my life. Normally my inner peace would be disturbed by the phone ringing during homeschool, John Mark needing attention when I was in the middle of disciplining his brothers, the computer malfunctioning while I was blogging, the boys picking up a virus on one of our few days out, complaints about dinner, backtalk, and disobedience. I made a commitment to accept these things and everything else that God allowed in my life.

I decided to whisper, "Jesus, I trust in you," whenever circumstances challenged me. I pictured myself kneeling at Jesus' feet like the Penitent Woman, opening my heart to his grace.

I still failed—often, in fact. But little by little, these acts of faith changed me. Little by little, I learned to acknowledge God's sovereignty over every moment of my day. Little by little, I sanctified the ordinary details of my day by doing nothing more than trusting.

Trying to accept with peace whatever happens during my day also taught me an unexpected lesson: I don't always want to do God's will.

Like so many other things, the words *I trust in you* are not magic. They are a prayer. They are an act of faith. They remind me to trust in God and ask for his help. But they can't make me trust when I don't want to. I have to open my heart. I have to work along with God's grace.

Sometimes I honestly tell the Lord, "Jesus, I trust in you—sort of." Like the man in the Gospel who said, "I believe; help my unbelief," (Mk 9:24), I pray, "Lord, I trust in you; help my lack of trust. Trust the Father for me. Trust his plan in me, when I am slow to surrender to him."

The late Fr. Thomas Dubay used to tell a story about St. Thomas Aquinas and his sister, who was a nun. One day, she came to the saint to ask him what she must do to become holy. St. Thomas answered with two words: "Will it."

We know that God offers us the grace to do his will. But his goodness goes beyond that. St. Paul wrote, "God is at work in you, *both to will and to work* for his good pleasure" (Phil 2:13, emphasis mine). In other words, God also offers us the grace to *desire* his will. We must open our hearts to receive it.

Since nothing but sin can separate us from the love of Christ, only one thing can keep us from being saints–our refusal to do God's will. God is all powerful, but there is one creature who can prevent him from sanctifying me–myself. Love cannot be forced. We must give it willingly.

This is part of what it means to trust God in the present. We must trust him more than our stubbornness, more than our sloth would lead us to. We must trust him when it goes against our instincts of self-preservation, when it seems that our way of dealing with a situation is better than his. He really does know best for us at every moment. He knows that the particular challenges we are facing right now are just what we need to grow in our trust and love. He offers us the strength to accept them. We must be willing to receive that strength.

It's hard—especially on the days when temptations come at us like arrows, one after another. I like to meditate on this verse: "Though an army encamp against me, my heart does not fear; Though war be waged against me, even then do I trust" (Ps 27:3). That is what I aspire to. But as a first step, I'd settle for remaining peaceful when my boys are waging raucous battles against each other.

Sanctification is not glamorous. We must embrace God's will right where we are today. Right where life is difficult or dull, where people misunderstand us or overlook our needs. We must constantly battle against ourselves. But we can win this battle. God fights by our side.

We can't fail, unless we give up

Despite my lack of will at times, that Lent was one of my best in years. Only a short time before I had felt like I couldn't succeed. Now I felt like I couldn't fail. What a revolution! If I failed to trust God originally, he offered me a second chance. If I became angry or anxious through a lack of trust, I could trust him to forgive me. And if I refused to repent immediately, he offered another chance in the next moment.

What was true for Lent is true for the rest of my life. I can grow in trust, no matter what—unless I give up, unless I stop trying.

God knows our weaknesses better than we do. He also knows how sincere we are. As long as we are trying, he doesn't see us as failures. He sees us as potential saints. And in order to become those saints, we have to trust him. Ultimately, he is in charge of our spiritual lives. Our natural gifts, our perfect practice of penance, or our perfect triumph over a particular sin can't earn us union with God. That is a gift. God will lead us down the specific path he has paved to get us there. We cannot fail, unless we give up.

Novice for life

By January of 1894, Therese had been in Carmel for five years. In the normal course of events, she would leave the novitiate in the fall.

When the time came, she asked for and received permission to remain there permanently. Therese chose to remain little, rather than growing up to be a full-fledged lay nun. She would take her place forever among the beginners. She could never fill an official office. She would follow the special schedule of those in formation, and even live in a special dormitory.

But she could do one thing the following year when she turned twenty-one that she had not been allowed to do before: she could fast. Her superiors would no longer pamper her with food.

She did invaluable work with the novices. Mother Marie de Gonzague silently acknowledged this. When Mother Marie was again elected prioress, she decided not to appoint a new novice mistress. She retained the title for herself, keeping Therese as her assistant.

Therese's littleness was beginning to affect the convent in new ways, as the novices learned from her how to abandon themselves to God's will. But her life soon took another turn. Less than two weeks after Marie de Gonzague reappointed her, Therese's tuberculosis manifested itself on the night after Good Friday prayers.

Questions for Reflection

1. What natural talents and spiritual gifts has God given me? How can I use them for his glory?

2. Do I envy others? Can I rejoice when someone else succeeds at something I have no talent in, or when others appear to have smooth roads to follow, while mine is beset with potholes?

Practical Suggestions

* If you are frustrated with a natural weakness, find a saint who struggled with the same problem and pray to him or her daily for inspiration and strength. Besides patron saints for almost every type of physical suffering, there are saints who suffered from alcoholism, personality problems, mental illness, etc.

* If you are gifted with a good imagination, choose a biblical image to picture along with, or in place of, a verbal act of faith to call to mind throughout the day. I picture myself as the Penitent Woman, laying my cheek on Jesus' foot. You might try picturing yourself as St. John the Apostle, leaning on Jesus' heart at the Last Supper, or a child being cradled in the arms of God the Father. Choose an image that communicates confidence in God.

Chapter Twelve
Hoping Against Hope

For I know the plans I have for you, says the LORD, plans for welfare and not for evil, to give you a future and a hope.

Jer 29:11

Although Therese experienced spiritual darkness for most of her time as a Carmelite, she learned to be at peace in its midst. She writes that in 1896, "I was saying to myself: Really I have no great exterior trials and for me to have interior ones, God would have to change my way" (SS 250).

The darkest night was yet to come. Early in the morning of Good Friday after taking her turn praying "before the Tomb," she returned upstairs to her cell in the St. Elijah dormitory of the novitiate.

There she performed the prescribed ritual for retiring. She took off her veil and close-fitting cap, carefully folding them and setting them on the bench beside her bed. She removed her scapular and knelt to kiss it. To gain an indulgence for sinners, she whispered, "O gloriosa Virginum, sublimis inter sidera . . ." ("Oh, glorious Virgin, enthroned above the stars . . .")

Rising, she folded the scapular, and added it to the pile of clothes. In its place she donned the little scapular for the night. Finally, she dipped her hand in holy water, sprinkled her bed with it, and knelt one more moment to commend her sleep to God. She was then free to extinguish the lamp and lie down.

Barely had Therese's head touched the pillow, when a rush of liquid poured out of her mouth. She stopped it with a handkerchief. Was it, as she thought, blood? Was this the first sure sign that she was seriously ill?

Not wanting to break the Rule, she remained in bed and coaxed herself to sleep. But with the first light of dawn she rose and brought the handkerchief to the shuttered window of her cell. Yes, it was blood!

In those days, tuberculosis was an incurable disease. It was a death sentence. Coughing up blood sometimes occurred with other diseases besides tuberculosis. But Therese had suspected for months that she was dying. Coughing up blood only confirmed her suspicions. She smiled to herself and prayed silently. She would soon see her Bridegroom face to face!

The next night she coughed up blood again.

Therese's joy in her illness was not to last. On Easter Sunday total spiritual darkness engulfed her, lasting until her death. Doubts about heaven assailed her.

Therese had always believed more fully in the existence of God than in the existence of atheists and agnostics. Life and God were inseparable! How could a person have one and not believe in the other? All that now changed. She was plunged into the spiritual abyss of those without any hope in a Savior. She felt no closeness to God, saw no light. As Jesus had eaten with sinners, Therese now saw herself as seated at table with them. She endured the pain of despair.

Writing to Mother Marie de Gonzague, she said an inner voice taunted her:

> You are dreaming about the light, about a fatherland embalmed in the sweetest perfumes, about the *eternal* possession of the Creator of all these marvels; you believe that one day you will walk out of the fog that surrounds you! Advance, advance; rejoice in the death

> which will give you not what you hope for but a night still more profound, the night of nothingness. (SS 213, emphasis in original)

Therese feared to speak or write much more than this about her darkness. She feared she might blaspheme. But more than once Mother Agnes recorded on scraps of paper that she asked her sister whether she was still in darkness. Each time the answer was *yes.*

How did Therese respond to this final assault against trust? "I turn my back on my adversaries without deigning to look them in the face," she wrote, "but I run toward my Jesus. I tell Him I am ready to shed my blood to the last drop to profess my belief in the existence of *heaven*" (ibid., emphasis in the original). At last she could experience pure joy, a joy having nothing to do with interior peace, but a truly selfless embrace of God's will.

Trusting God like Abraham

This chapter returns to the story of Abraham and his seemingly foolish hope. We'll discuss the darkness of unanswered prayers and hope for the conversion of sinners. I'll share how turning forty intensified my psychological distress, and the unexpected events that followed. We'll see how Therese's last consolations were taken from her.

In this final darkness, Therese again trusted God after the pattern of Abraham. The New Testament speaks extensively of Abraham's example in Romans 4 and Hebrews 11.

When God promised Abraham that Sarah would bear a son,

> No distrust made him waver concerning the promise of God, but he grew strong in his faith as he gave glory to God, fully convinced that God was able to do what he had promised. (Rom 4:20–21)

Sarah gave birth to a son and she and Abraham named him Isaac. But God was not done teaching Abraham to trust. God spoke to him again, saying,

> Take your son, your only son Isaac, whom you love, and go to the land of Mori'ah, and offer him there as a burnt offering upon one of the mountains of which I shall tell you. (Gn 22:2)

Amazingly, Abraham did not hesitate, although he must have been shocked and heartbroken. God had said his promises would be fulfilled through Isaac. How could this be, if Isaac was to die?

The New Testament interprets this story for us. "[Abraham] considered that God was able to raise men even from the dead" (Heb 11:19). Abraham refused to doubt God's promises, no matter what. If an unheard-of miracle was necessary to fulfill them, God would perform it. This was centuries before the prophet Elijah. Up to this point in salvation history, no one had ever been raised from the dead!

"In hope he believed against hope" (Rom 4:18). On a human level, Abraham hoped unreasonably, but that did not stop him. He talked to God as a man talks to his friend, just as Moses did later. He ate with God and his angels, and bargained with him over the fate of Sodom and Gomorrah. He understood that God was faithful, and he was convinced that God would never disappoint him.

Just when Abraham took up his knife to slay Isaac, an angel stopped him. "Do not lay your hand on the lad or do anything to him; for now I know that you fear God, seeing you have not withheld your son, your only son, from me" (Gn 22:12). God restored Isaac to him.

God's promise to Abraham and his descendants could still be fulfilled through the son Sarah had miraculously born. Abraham did not live to see his descendants inherit the Promised Land. In fact, the writer to the Hebrews says that God finally fulfilled this promise in Christ, thousands of years later. But Abraham did not have to see in order to believe. Nothing shook his trust.

Like Abraham, Therese hoped against hope. Even though doubts besieged her about the reality of heaven, she proclaimed she would willingly die for her belief in it. She knew that God would fulfill his promises to her. She did not let spiritual darkness rob her of her trust. Instead, her trust grew stronger.

Like Abraham's trust, Therese's appeared unreasonable. We marvel at it. But Therese—and Abraham, who is, after all, our father—would have us imitate it! St. Paul likewise writes:

> We rejoice in our hope of the glory of God. More than that, we rejoice in our sufferings, knowing that suffering produces endurance, and endurance produces character, and character produces hope, and hope does not disappoint us, because God's love has been poured into our hearts through the Holy Spirit who has been given to us. (Rom 5:3–5)

Trust begins with love. The Holy Spirit infuses love into our hearts at Baptism, along with faith and hope. The closer we grow to God in prayer, the more he infuses Jesus' love and faithfulness into us.

Therese desired to love God back with his own love, because she knew that mere human love was inadequate. On her own, she could never love God as he deserved to be loved. She could never love him as he loved her. But she used what love she had for him to give herself completely over to him. She entrusted herself to God in the little ways that she could, and he proved faithful. This increased her confidence in his love and goodness and drew her ever closer to him. God pushed her trust to the very limit, so that she could reach the highest limits of love.

When your prayers go unanswered

What should we do when we are in the midst of a seemingly hopeless situation? Many of us have been praying for the same intention for years with no discernible answer. Why does God turn a deaf ear to our cries? Doesn't he care?

In our day nearly everyone has a loved one (or several) who has left the Church or is living in mortal sin. Our heart aches to think that this person might be eternally lost. The pain is especially deep when the lost person is a close family member. We pray and sacrifice every day, but he comes no closer to God, as far as we can tell.

Let us not give up! God will come through for us. I firmly believe that God will answer our prayers for our loved ones to be saved. We can never trust God too much. If we place complete trust in him, miracles will occur, as they did for Abraham. Let us offer our loved ones to God. Let us believe that he can raise them from the death of sin, even as Abraham believed God could raise Isaac.

Speaking about her work with the novices, Therese said, "We must fight unwearyingly to win the battle, even if we are without hope" (HF 325). God changes hearts. We can only persevere. If we persist in doing our part, can we not trust God to do his?

The conversion of a murderer

Before Therese received permission to enter Carmel, when she was just learning to trust God, she wanted to bring souls to him through her prayers. She heard about a notorious, unrepentant murderer who was soon to be hanged. Henri Pranzini killed two women and a twelve-year-old girl in an apparent robbery. The entire country was talking about the case. Therese took him up as her mission. She prayed and sacrificed for him daily, and recruited Celine to join her.

They did not just offer God their good works for Pranzini. They offered the merits of Jesus and all the treasures of the Church to God the Father on his behalf. They had a Mass said for his conversion.

> I felt in the depths of my heart *certain* that our desires would be granted, but to obtain courage to pray for sinners I told God I was sure He would pardon the poor, unfortunate Pranzini; that I'd believe this even if he went to his death without *any signs of repentance* or without *having gone to confession.* I was absolutely confident in the mercy of Jesus. But I was begging Him for a *"sign"* of repentance only for my own simple consolation. (SS 100, emphasis in the original)

Therese read the newspaper to keep up with the case, looking for the public sign that her prayers had been answered. Up to the day of his execution, the prisoner remained unyielding. He refused to go to confession. Then at the last minute on the scaffold itself, he turned and three times kissed a crucifix that a priest held out to him. God had heard their prayers!

Zeal to convert sinners filled Therese's soul. Jesus thirsted for souls on whom to bestow his mercy. The more Therese satisfied his thirst with her sacrifices and prayers, the more she thirsted to offer them.

We do not know the mysterious plans of God. Perhaps our struggle to hope against hope is the very sacrifice that will save our loved one's soul.

Remember how Therese said God would not give us desires that he did not mean to fulfill? I hold onto this truth, not just for myself, but for everyone I love. Would God give us hope for their salvation and not fulfill it? God desires their conversion more than we do. "As I live, says the Lord GOD, I have no pleasure in the death of the wicked, but that the wicked turn from his way and live" (Ez 33:11).

And the Apostle says, "The Lord is not slow about his promise as some count slowness, but is forbearing toward you, not wishing that any should perish, but that all should reach repentance" (1 Pet 3:9). Like the people of the Old Testament, we may die without seeing the fruits of our prayers. But that's no reason to give up hope. Think how much more efficacious our prayers will be in heaven!

What about free will? God will not force anyone to come to him. Does that mean we can only cross our fingers, but not have true hope? I believe we can go further than that. The Church teaches that God sometimes bestows efficacious grace on his children. Efficacious grace always accomplishes what God intends it to do. If he gives the efficacious grace of conversion to a sinner, that sinner will necessarily repent and turn to him. We do not know for certain how efficacious grace works along with free will. Different theological schools have different explanations. Free will remains a mystery. But God *can* ensure that a sinner repents without overriding the person's free will. This we know.

God wants us to trust him. He will be faithful. He delights in the audacity of the saints. He will delight in ours. Our faith in his goodness will move mountains. It will save souls.

Has one of our loved ones already passed away with no sign of penitence? We should not despair. Only God knows what happened secretly in his final moments. And the deceased may need our prayers in Purgatory.

What if our prayer is for a cure that never materializes a job offer that never comes, or a lost child who is never found? God's silence challenges our faith. Still we strive to believe that his ways *are* best, that all *shall* be made well.

In the meantime, we suffer. We protest that we don't want to be sanctified at the expense of our loved one's health or life. We tell God we would rather remain as we are and have peace and love in this life. But would we really?

God knows our hearts better than we do. He fashioned them. He knows what will truly satisfy us. This saying of St. Augustine's has been heard so often, it has become a cliché, but it is still true: "You have made us for yourself, O Lord, and our hearts are restless until they rest in thee."

Moving beyond hopelessness

In the midst of my fears for my children and the future of our country, I was also struggling with other issues. My fortieth birthday was unexpectedly difficult. In my younger, inexperienced years, I rolled my eyes when people spoke of mid-life crises or difficulties with growing older. *What's the big deal?* I thought. *Why can't people just accept their age? We're all growing older all the time.* I had no plans for using anti-aging creams or dying my hair. I looked forward to eternal life with God, so why would aging bother me?

When my fortieth birthday arrived, we were in the second of two years when many old friends, acquaintances, or their loved ones passed away, including the suicide I wrote about earlier. The day brought death even more to the fore. Wrinkles at the corners of my eyes and strands of gray hair appeared, seemingly all at once. I felt like I had gone nowhere spiritually for twenty years.

At the same time, I feared that my childbearing years were over. We conceived our first three children almost on demand. But now Carlo was nineteen months old. We tried for months to conceive again with no success. My body was slowing down. The prospect of more children, which both Dan and I desired, was dwindling. We discussed adopting a daughter, but we had no idea how we could afford it while Dan worked for the Church.

I had always loved birthdays until then. I tried to put on a happy face for my family. Dan was bringing home take-out Chinese food and cheesecake to celebrate. While he was at work, I fought back tears.

I feel like all the good things in life are past, I said, half to myself, half to God. *Marriage, having children . . . What is there to look forward to?*

I felt guilty complaining about not having more than three children, when so many couples could not conceive at all. But I also felt like our family was incomplete. I hadn't expected to be moving on to a new stage of life so soon.

Somehow I made it through the day without a complete breakdown.

This sadness and distress lurked in the background for the next year. Then Dan broached a subject we had discussed many times before—his looking for a new job. I hated the work of moving and of having to start over making friends. Since both of us were introverted, it was difficult to keep pulling up roots. I always thought we would be settled in one place long before this age, as both sets of our parents were.

I feared that if we moved and Dan continued working for the Church, we would have to live farther from our families. As we entered middle age, our parents entered their seventies. We both wanted our boys to know their grandparents, and we hoped to spend as much time with our parents as we could while they were still around.

On the other hand, I knew Dan was bored at work. He made many changes in his office over the six years we had lived in La Crosse. Now he felt there were no new challenges ahead for him. An even larger issue was our financial situation. Dan had spent most of his adult life in graduate school or in the employ of a diocese. I had been a foreign missionary, and was now staying at home full time. We had little savings for our retirement, which suddenly loomed before us.

Dan's happiness is one of my top priorities. Perhaps my own struggles helped me be more open than I was in the past. This time when he brought up the subject I said, "Well, if it's God's will, we just have to do it. Let's see what jobs are available."

Dan sat down at the computer in our family room and began visiting electronic billboards with Catholic job postings. Immediately he found a position open in New Ulm, Minnesota. Not only was New Ulm over fifty miles closer to our families than La Crosse, it was also the hometown of Dan's mother. Dan remembered visiting his grandfather in New Ulm when he was little. Extended family still lived there.

We also knew the new bishop, John LeVoir, by reputation. He co-authored a well-known book on the Theology of the Body. He had also been pastor at Dan's sister's parish before being appointed bishop.

Dan decided to apply for the job before he looked any further. A short time later he accepted the job offer, and we began packing to move back to Minnesota.

Life with God is an adventure. We need to keep moving forward, seeking and doing his will, rather than letting fear or despair freeze us in place. We can never know ahead of time all the good things that God has planned for us.

After we bought our house in New Ulm, we learned that our next-door neighbors homeschool their children, whose ages are similar to ours. Since then, another Catholic family down the street has started home-schooling too. We have a much more active homeschooling group here than we had in Wisconsin, which makes a big difference for me and the kids.

But the greatest surprise God had in store was the birth of our fourth son two years after the move. We had long given up the hope of more children before we knew John Mark was on the way. God can bring new life—physically or spiritually—into every situation.

I could have kept my focus on myself and been bitter, leaving Dan unhappy as well. I could have missed the opportunity to be closer to our families and to make some wonderful new friends. I thank God for the grace to be open, in spite of myself. Life at forty-six is nothing like my forty-year-old self imagined.

Looking towards eternity

Hopelessness does not just stem from tragic situations. Each stage of life has its unique temptations to despair. Adolescents struggle with not fitting in and being misunderstood and rejected. Young adults wonder if they will ever find a satisfying job or a spouse. Middle-aged adults fear they have made the wrong decisions in life and that it's too late to change. Older adults watch as friends and family die, and experience their own decline in health.

Despair can proceed from the little disappointments of daily life, as well as from life's tragedies. When we place our hope in God and view our lives from an eternal perspective, every moment has meaning. Boredom can sanctify us. Domestic duties can purify our love. Financial woes can help us see God as our true treasure. The smallest act gains eternal significance when done out of love for God. Every moment is pregnant with adventure, for it hides within itself the seed of good triumphing over evil. We must cooperate with God in order for that seed to be born, though the labor causes us to wail.

The journey of trust does not end until death. The battle rages till the end. God alone will be our strength.

Heaven is eternal—think of that! Our sufferings here, no matter how great, will one day be over. That's why St. Paul could write, "I consider that the sufferings of this present time are not worth comparing with the glory about to be revealed to us" (Rom 8:18).

God loves us and our loved ones with an infinite love. If we believe, we will see the glory of God, as Martha did when Jesus raised her brother Lazarus from the dead (see Jn 11:1–43). Let us not allow circumstances to persuade us to think differently.

If we let him, God will purify us of everything that holds us back from him—even things that may seem good to us. He alone knows the depths of purification we need.

Trusting in God, rather than his promises

Therese realized that her desire for heaven was partly natural, a desire for eternal life, rather than a longing to see God face-to-face. She believed God had sent this deepest darkness to complete her purification. She would offer all her suffering for sinners.

> What anyone says to me about death no longer penetrates; it slides over me as it would over smooth glass. It's finished! The hope of death is all used up. Undoubtedly God does not will that I think of it as I did before I became sick. At that time, this thought was necessary for me and very profitable; I really felt it. But today it's just the contrary. God wills that I abandon myself like a very little child who is not disturbed by what others will do to him. (LC 65)

Therese recalled how her mother had dragged herself to daily Mass almost until the end of her life. She had only reluctantly given up her duties when she could no longer fulfill them. Therese wished she herself had told no one about the course of her disease, not even the infirmarian. She would have preferred to continue working, continue praying with the community. But one by one she had to let go of every activity. As her breath grew shorter and her strength disappeared, she could no longer even recite the Offices for the Dead.

For the last several months of her life, Therese received the Sacred Host with difficulty. Many times she was obviously too ill to receive Communion. At other times, her sisters offered her the possibility of Communion and she did not want to say *no*. She secretly wished one of her superiors would forbid her to receive. She hesitated to suggest this herself. She knew the Eucharist strengthened her spiritually, yet her continuing bloody coughs, vomiting, and struggling for breath made her fear that she would commit some kind of sacrilege with the Host.

At last on August 20, 1897, she couldn't stop crying over the matter. Her sobs were literally choking her. She avoided meeting her sisters' gaze. Mother Agnes guessed what the trouble was and gently asked her about it. In the yellow notebook in which she later transcribed her notes on Therese's final months, she writes, "I consoled her as well as I could, and she seemed close to dying of sorrow. Never had I seen her in such agony" (LC 157).

God denied Therese this final consolation. Still, her agony did not stop her from stating, "Without doubt, it is a great grace to receive the sacraments, but when the good God does not permit it, it is good, all the same" (STL 180).

At last it was impossible for her to do any works at all. She could no longer gain merit for souls through prayer or sacrifices. She asked Jesus to do so in her place. She could only suffer with love. She was living by pure trust and nothing else.

Questions for Reflection

1. What prayers have I been waiting a long time for God to answer? Are there any practical steps I can take to move things forward?

2. Have I lost hope for the future?

Practical Suggestions

* If you are feeling hopeless, find someone trustworthy who can support you. Can you open up to your spouse, a parent, a close friend, or a priest?

* Make a list of all the good surprises God has brought into your life over the years. Remind yourself that you really don't know what the future holds.

* Find a quiet place where you can unburden your soul before God each day. Praying before the Blessed Sacrament may help lift your burden.

* If you are praying for a lost loved one, cultivate a devotion to St. Monica. She prayed for her non-Christian son for years. He eventually converted and we now know him as St. Augustine.

Chapter Thirteen
Trust and the Four Last Things

Consider the ancient generations and see: who ever trusted in the Lord and was put to shame?

Sir 2:10

On June 3, Mother Marie de Gonzague, at the suggestion of Mother Agnes, ordered Therese to write more about her little way. This became Manuscript C of *Story of a Soul.* Therese brought the manuscript to the infirmary on July 8, to continue writing as long as she could. Soon she was too weak to hold a pen. Instead of quitting, she switched to using a pencil. Sometime later that month, even that was too much for her. Her hand shook, and at last, the pencil trailed off the page with this sentenced unfinished: "It is not because God, in His anticipating Mercy, has preserved my soul from mortal sin that I go to Him with confidence and love . . ." (SS 259).

In the infirmary, Therese continued to cough up blood daily. On July 30, Dr. de Corniere thought death was imminent, as he had once before. Besides almost constant bloody coughing, Therese was suffocating. The next evening, Cannon Maupas came and at last gave her the final sacraments. Meanwhile, the nuns prepared for her death and burial.

In the next room, the sacristans gathered candles, holy water, and a straw mattress on which to place her body after death. They left the door open, and Therese saw what they were doing. Even now, her humor remained. "You see that candle over there," she said to Sr. Genevieve, "when the divine thief comes to take me it will be put in my hand, but you must not give me the candlestick, it is too ugly" (SL 198).

For several days Therese remained in this state. The doctor thought she might die at any moment. Then she stabilized again on August 5. She was still terribly weak and in pain, but her coughing stopped. After having trouble digesting anything for weeks, she now craved all sorts of food. The nuns in the kitchen tried to supply whatever she asked for—from roast beef to chocolate éclairs.

Dr. de Corniere did not know what to make of this. Assuming that her death was going to be delayed after all, he left town and advised the Guerins that they too could travel for the sake of Isidore's health.

Once her condition stabilized, Therese again asked for a pencil. She did not wish to return to her manuscript, but she wanted to write to Fr. Belliere one last time. The first time she asked, Mother Agnes would not give her permission. But on August 25, she allowed Therese to write. Therese dedicated a holy card to Fr. Belliere as a "last souvenir." The card has these words: "I cannot fear a God who made himself so little for me . . . I love him . . . For He is but love and mercy" (LT 266, punctuation in the original).

Then Therese's dreadful sufferings returned. Her legs swelled. The tuberculosis attacked her intestines, causing excruciating pain. Again she was suffocating.

She had one more period of calm before the final crisis, which lasted from September 13 to 30. Dr. Francis La Neele, husband of her cousin Jeanne Guerin, examined Therese in Dr. de Corniere's absence. He marveled that she was still alive. Her right lung was completely gone, and only a small portion of her left lung remained.

Empty hands

This chapter brings us to the end of our study of trust. It centers on the four last things: death, judgment, heaven, and hell. We will return to the theme of merit, as we ask why God dragged Therese's suffering out for so long. We will examine her teaching on Purgatory. We'll discuss the Last Judgment from the perspective of trust. I'll share how I had to leave the Carmelite Order. And we'll encounter a final, surprising peril on our road to trusting God.

We read about the suffering Therese endured and may be tempted again to ask *why?* Why, when Dr. de Corniere had forecast her death back in June, did God keep Therese alive for over three more months? She suffered almost constantly during those months. Why must she hang on and on, even telling her sisters that if she were not a Christian, she would not have hesitated to commit suicide, she was enduring so much pain?

Was God giving her a chance to store up merits for heaven, in order to receive more glory there? No. Therese put aside her sacrifice beads long ago. She not only stopped counting her merits, she stopped hording them as well.

On June 9, 1895, Therese set down her thoughts about the Last Judgment. She offered herself as a victim to God's love, writing her famous Act of Oblation to Merciful Love:

> After earth's Exile, I hope to go and enjoy You in the Fatherland, but I do not want to lay up merits for heaven. I want to work for Your *Love alone* with the one purpose of pleasing You, consoling Your Sacred Heart, and saving souls who will love You eternally.
>
> In the evening of this life, I shall appear before You with empty hands, for I do not ask You, Lord, to count my works. All our justice is stained in Your eyes. I wish, then, to be clothed in Your own *Justice* and to receive from Your *Love* the eternal possession of *Yourself*. I want no other *Throne*, no other *Crown*, but *You*, my *Beloved!* (SS 277, emphasis in the original)

We learn three things about Therese's spirituality and trust from this self-offering. First, she performed little acts of love, not to gain merits for herself, but to offer them to God to apply to sinners. She had rejoiced in doing this since first praying for Pranzini as a teenager. "I don't know whether I'll go to Purgatory or not, but I'm not in the least bit disturbed about it," she told Mother Agnes, "however, if I do go there, I'll not regret having done nothing to avoid it. I shall not be sorry for having worked solely for the salvation of souls" (LC 56).

Every pain she endured, she offered for others. Her prolonged passion was God's answer to her prayer to save sinners.

Second, Therese missed no opportunity of making little sacrifices. She did this not out of fear, but freely, out of love. She knew she personally gained nothing from her efforts.

Finally, she often repeated that she would not mind going to Purgatory. If she did go there, she would follow the lead of Shadrach, Meshach, and Abednego, singing hymns in the flames. This too she would gladly endure for others' sake (LC 81.)

But she hoped to go straight to heaven, despite her lack of merit. One day Mother Agnes lamented that she herself had no good works to offer to God on Judgment Day. Therese replied that she was "in the same circumstances." But Therese rejoiced in this. Since she could give God nothing, he would supply everything (LC 67).

> As far as little ones are concerned, they will be judged with great gentleness. . . . "At the end, the Lord will rise up to save the gentle and the humble of the earth." It doesn't say "to judge"; but "to save". (LC 199, punctuation in the original)

She confirmed what she had told her cousin Marie back in July. Those who trust God fully cannot go to Purgatory. Since they rely on

God alone for their salvation, he will supply whatever is lacking to bring them swiftly to himself.

Facing our Judge without fear

How can we trust God concerning Judgment Day as Therese did? We fear death. We fear facing God and having our sins and weaknesses exposed before the world. We know we fall short, and we suspect our sinfulness is much worse than we realize.

Even if we have committed mortal sin in our lifetime, we only have to fear God in one circumstance—if we die unrepentant, or with no intention of confessing our sin as soon as possible.

When I begin to doubt the depths of God's mercy, I can look back on my relationship with Dan as a guide to approaching Judgment Day.

After Dan and I met through Single Catholics Online, we sent e-mails to each other for a few weeks, and then talked for hours on the phone. Before long we decided it was time to meet in person.

As I prepared for our first date, my hands shook from nervousness. I had so few dating experiences before this, and none of them had seemed as important as that Saturday evening in July 2000. I didn't know if I was ready to see Dan face to face. His younger sister was due to have a baby that month. The impending birth and Baptism provided an excuse for him to come home from Washington, D.C. He could spend a few weeks in the Twin Cities and get to know me in person without anyone else thinking too much about it.

In preparation for our date I had my hair cut in a layered bob as in my Single Catholics Online profile picture, which was a few years old. I donned a black velvet T-shirt and brown slacks for the evening, and fastened a silver cross pendant around my neck. I tried to calm my nerves by telling myself, "There's nothing to worry about. It's just Dan."

Dan and I had enjoyed our conversations. We already knew a lot about each other. We were friends. From the start we were completely genuine with each other, rather than acting a part. What did I have to fear? If God's plan didn't include a deepening of our relationship, that wouldn't happen. I knew Dan would not reject me as a person. Most (I'll admit–not all) of my nervousness disappeared at these thoughts.

Of course, that date went better than I had imagined it would, eventually leading to our marriage eleven months later.

God knows me better than my husband does now, let alone at the start of our relationship. God sees inside my heart. "You discern my purpose from afar," wrote the psalmist (Ps 139:2). God never misjudges me. He judges me both justly and mercifully. That comforts me and gives me peace.

Therese wrote, "I hope as much from the Justice of the Good God as from His Mercy. . . . I do not understand those souls who fear so tender a Friend" (LT 226). And elsewhere, "What a sweet joy it is to think that God is *Just,* i.e., that He takes into account our weakness, that He is perfectly aware of our fragile nature" (SS 180).

Every time I read these lines, I think of these words of the title character of *Anne of Green Gables:* "I chatter on far too much. But if you only knew how many things I want to say and don't, you'd give me some credit" (L. M. Montgomery. New York: Grosset and Dunlap, 1983, 303).

God knows how many things we want to say and don't—out of love for him. He sees all the temptations we overcome, not just those we give in to. He sees our resolutions, our weakness, the illness or lack of sleep or stress or sorrow that break down our defenses. Others may judge us too harshly—God, never. His judgment includes all the good in our souls, as well as all the bad. He gives us the credit for them. Unless we, like Therese, choose to give that credit away.

What then? If we give away all our merits, will he only see the bad in our souls on Judgment Day? Sr. Marie of the Trinity, who had a great fear of Purgatory, posed this question to Therese. She replied:

> Do not say that! Our Lord is Justice itself, and if He does not judge our good actions, neither will He judge our bad ones. It seems to me, that for Victims of Love there will be no judgment. God will rather hasten to reward with eternal delights His own Love which He will behold burning in their hearts. (*Counsels and Reminiscences*, online at goodcatholicbooks.org/therese.html, translator unknown; punctuation in the original)

Is it hope or presumption?

One of Therese's companions in the novitiate was Sr. Marie-Philomene, who was forty-five at the time of Therese's entrance. This sister had entered Carmel years before, but had left because she felt it was her duty to attend to her mother, who was unexpectedly dying. Afterwards, Marie-Philomene desired to re-enter Carmel, but Mother Genevieve, the foundress of the Lisieux Carmel, would not allow it. Finally, after a lapse of nine years, Mother Marie de Gonzague was able to obtain permission for her re-entry.

Perhaps Marie-Philomene took her idea of God's character from this severe treatment. She also had a great fear of Purgatory. Therese told her:

> You're not confident enough, you have too much fear of the Good God; I assure you he is grieved by it. Do not fear Purgatory because of the pain you would suffer there but desire to not go to make God happy who imposes this expiation with so much regret. Therefore when you seek to please him in everything, if you have unshakeable confidence that he is purifying you every in-

> stant in his love and leaving no trace of sin in you; be sure that you won't go to Purgatory. (NPPO of Sr. Marie-Philomene)

This instruction gives us the key. We must "seek to please [God] in everything." Therese leaves no room for lazy, half-hearted efforts. Her dealings with the novices bear this out. We cannot simply state we are going to bypass Purgatory and leave it at that. Wishing will not make it so. That is not the little way.

Recall the words of the *Catechism:* "All subsequent sin [after Adam's] would be disobedience toward God and lack of trust in his goodness" (397). When we sin deliberately, we manifest our mistrust.

In order to go straight to heaven, we must tirelessly seek to do God's will. On the other hand, it is *seeking*, not *succeeding* that matters. God does not expect us to be successful at combating sin on our own. He only expects us to fight temptation. Some sins are committed through weakness, not premeditated. Wounded and weak, each of us may have an area where we continue to fall, even though we are trying. We may continue to struggle for years, even until our last day on earth. God will make up for our lack of success in these areas, if we trust in him. In fact, our failures might be necessary in his plan to lead us to greater humility and trust.

Our confidence must be "unshakeable." Can we hope against hope, even against the evidence of our eyes and hearts, even if everyone around us opposes our trust? We should not, of course, close our ears to caution coming from spiritual directors and others in authority over us. Perhaps God sent them to point out how much work we have left to do. But in the end, only God's judgment matters. He is the only one whose judgment never errs.

God's purifying love can remove all trace of sin in this life. We know this already, but few of us have gone as far as Therese did, believing that it will happen to us. Even after we accept the teaching that our works cannot earn us heaven, we cling to the belief that they alone can spare us from Purgatory. Then we see how poor our works are, and we falter. We give up the hope of going directly to heaven. How can we possibly avoid all sin? Or earn enough merit to balance the weight of our sin?

But we know now that "it is trust" and not great deeds "that must bring us to Love." So why do we doubt? Do we secretly think the way of trust is too hard? Are we still, despite our protests to the contrary, focusing on ourselves?

If we can hope against hope for the salvation of our loved ones, not giving in to doubt and despair even when they die without any public sign of repentance, we can also hope against hope for ourselves. At the very last moment, as we take our last breath, God can remove the burden that has weighed us down for so long. He can remove the temporal punishment due to our sin at the same time. Dare we trust that he will do so? Dare we be as audacious as Therese, hoping for life where we only see death?

Therese wrote to Fr. Roulland that, if souls who trusted God perfectly still appear before him without being perfectly pure, the Blessed Virgin will step forward to aid them. She will grant them the grace of making a perfect act of love, which will immediately purify them of everything. Then they can enter heaven at once (LT 226).

Everyone can achieve perfect trust in God! Therefore, everyone can go directly to heaven. Everyone can be a saint. No, it is not easy to trust at every moment, but it is possible. And this is the way God meant the Christian life to be. When we resign ourselves to Purgatory, we aim too low. Purgatory is a last mercy for those who cling to their works and to creatures. But God does not want us to go there. He desires to sanctify us completely here and now.

Jesus prayed, "I thank thee, Father, Lord of heaven and earth, that thou hast hidden these things from the wise and understanding and revealed them to babes" (Mt 11:25). We don't have to be wise to avoid Purgatory. We don't need brilliant intellects. These things can hinder us. Our minds cannot pierce the heavens. When it comes to the Four Last Things—death, judgment, heaven, and hell—we need to become babies, who trust their Father for everything.

Will everyone go straight to heaven?

We have probably all been at funerals where the deceased is "canonized" by the priest or eulogists. "We know he is with God, because he lived such a good life," they say. But do we?

What does the Church say?

> All who die in God's grace and friendship, but still imperfectly purified, are indeed assured of their eternal salvation; but after death they undergo purification, so as to achieve the holiness necessary to enter the joy of heaven. (CCC 1030)

Everyone who is not perfectly purified on this earth will have to go through Purgatory in order to enter heaven. Only God can determine whether someone has been perfectly purified. Our prayers can help souls in Purgatory to be purified more quickly. We don't want to deprive our loved ones of this help out of a mistaken notion about the state of their souls.

What if someone truly trusts God in the manner Therese did? Are we doubting God's goodness and wasting time with our prayers when we pray for them? To answer the second question first, we believe that if a soul has already entered heaven, God will use our prayers to help another soul in Purgatory for whom no one is praying. So our prayers for the dead are never wasted, and may even be an act of charity towards a stranger. Since we cannot read another person's soul, we should leave distribution of the benefits of our prayers to God.

Since Therese's day, some theologians have asked whether God condemns anyone to hell. Since God is all merciful, "dare we hope" that he will offer the efficacious grace of conversion to all, even at the last moment?

Therese's daring view of avoiding Purgatory might seem to support such a hope. But let's not assume too much. Therese never proposed that Purgatory was empty, let alone hell. She did not concern herself with universal principles, but with individual choices. She believed some Christians, even some saints, spent time in Purgatory. If they did not trust God for everything, their works would be weighed in the balance—not determining whether they would ultimately enter heaven, of course, but determining how much purification they would need.

Sr. Febronie served as sub-prioress during Therese's early years in Carmel. She reproached Therese for teaching the novices that they could go straight to heaven after death, calling this presumption. "My sister, if you desire God's justice, you will have God's justice," Therese answered her. "The soul receives exactly what she looks for from God" (NPPA of Sr. Marie of the Angels; my translation.)

This conversation took place in 1891. The following January, Febronie was among those who died during the flu epidemic. She appeared to Therese in a dream a short time later. Therese saw Febronie was suffering. She looked as though she was confirming that Therese had been right. She was in Purgatory, because she had expected to receive God's justice rather than his mercy.

Here once more we see the importance of our participation in our sanctification. God even allows us to choose the method by which he will judge us! If we believe he will send us to Purgatory because we have not been good enough, then he will. If we trust him to make up for our lack of perfection, he will do that instead.

Leaving Carmel

If we desire to rely completely on God and nothing else, he will detach us from everything that we have wrongly trusted in. Sometimes, as I have experienced, our trust is in the means to holiness, instead of the end, God himself.

In June 2002, I hobbled to the front of St. Michael's Church in West St. Paul, Minnesota. Dan was in the back of the Church, swinging five-day-old Dante in his car seat to keep him from crying. There, before a congregation consisting of my parents and many other Secular Carmelites and their families, I pronounced these words: "Inspired by the Holy Spirit, and in response to God's call, I, Mary Francis of the Divine Mercy, sincerely promise to the Superiors of the Order of Teresian Carmel, and to you, my brothers and sisters, to tend toward evangelical perfection in the spirit of the evangelical counsels of chastity, poverty, and obedience, and of the Beatitudes, according to the Rule of the Secular Order of Discalced Carmelites, for the rest of my life. . . ."

The journey I had begun in 1993 when I read *How to Avoid Purgatory* was reaching its fulfillment.

The Twin Cities had an usually large number of OCDS communities. When Dan and I moved to an apartment in West St. Paul a few months after our marriage, we transferred to a community that met at a nearby parish. A year or two later, that community spilt in two, with half following the priest who was the spiritual assistant to his new parish in another suburb. We moved to this new community, even though it meant a longer travel time to meetings.

Starting in the fall after my definitive promise, our whole family attended monthly Carmelite meetings together. Dan was a novice, studying to make his first promise. We sat in the cry room during Afternoon and

Evening Prayer, and Eucharistic Adoration. I nursed Dante. Dan took notes as the community's spiritual assistant taught from Teresa of Avila's writings. Although ours was not the ideal way to pray or to study, we did the best we could with an infant.

The following spring, we moved to La Crosse. We were 170 miles from our Carmelite community. We still attempted to attend meetings for the first year and more. Clerical errors left Dan without a chance to make his first promise and he decided to quietly leave, rather than make a fuss.

In the meantime, the president of our new community phoned me to say the group had been formed without proper permission from the provincial delegate in charge of OCDS members in our area. The council was shutting down the community and transferring elsewhere. The community that had remained in West St. Paul was without a required spiritual assistant. Transferring back there was not a good option.

I sought to transfer to a community that was fifteen minutes closer to home. After I visited, some long-time members there complained that my nursing baby was too noisy for their elderly ears. I could not attend meetings without him. Another community limited new members to one per formation year. I did not want to take the only available spot, when I didn't know if I would be able to come to every monthly meeting.

Then I received a phone call from another member of our community, assuring me the last phone call had been wrong. Our group was going to continue to meet. We just needed to elect a new council. Any problems between the community and the order were being worked out. Since the remaining communities in the Twin Cities were even farther away from our home, I decided to stay put and hope for the best.

In time, travelling to the Twin Cities for meetings became too difficult for our family. It left us no time for visiting with our parents and siblings. For four to six months of the year, the weather also presented difficulties.

I studied along with my formation class by correspondence, and spoke by phone with the president or formation director of the community a few times a year.

Our OCDS community was very understanding as long as we lived in La Crosse. Many members were astonished that we even tried to attend meetings. But when we moved to New Ulm, that attitude changed. Although we still lived well over an hour from the Twin Cities, the fact that our address was in Minnesota altered other Carmelites' expectations. They wanted me to come to meetings regularly again. I too hoped that would be possible.

Dan thought the burden of travel, especially through open countryside, too great. Family considerations also came into play. We had routinely stayed with Dan's parents while in the Twin Cities. They were now experiencing health issues. We hesitated to place any burdens on them. If their house was not open to us, what would Dan do with three little boys while I spent hours at the meetings?

I sought advice from an OCDS member who was active at the provincial level. She presented my case to the provincial delegate to the Secular Carmelites. He granted me a temporary exemption from attending meetings. So, for another eighteen months I e-mailed my formation homework to our community.

Then in an unexpected e-mail, I received a copy of a letter the provincial delegate sent to our president. The Discalced Carmelite friars had decided to suppress our community. Meetings halted immediately. Any members desiring to remain in the order were told to transfer to another community in the Twin Cities. As always, those communities would choose whether or not to accept each prospective transfer. The provincial delegate required the communities to delay decisions on acceptance for one year. He was concerned about the level of formation we had received. During that time, we had to attend meetings faithfully.

I did not like the idea of transferring to another community. I had tried that before. John Mark was on the way, and I could imagine my request being rejected again because of a happy, noisy baby. Besides, how could I commit to attending all meetings over the next year when I would have a newborn?

I e-mailed the provincial delegate privately, reminding him of the exception he made for me in the past. I hoped he would extend it. He replied that now I was without a community, so that exception was withdrawn. I had to follow the same directions he gave everyone else. If that was not possible for me . . . He let me complete the sentence.

I could no longer be faithful to my Carmelite promise.

I printed out his e-mail and sat on the couch in our living room, reading it over and over. Mentally, I paced the floor with my hands in my hair. Must I ask to be released from my promise? I had not made it lightly. I had sacrificed to get to the profession ceremony, only two days after being released from the hospital following my difficult C-section. We had also sacrificed to attend meetings as long as we could. I had fully intended to remain an OCDS member for life.

How was I ever going to become holy without the graces that came to me through the Carmelite Order? I wanted to be buried in the large scapular. I wanted the order to pray and offer Masses for me when I died. I wanted to wear the Carmelite habit in heaven. I wanted to think of Teresa of Avila as my mother, John of the Cross as my father, and Therese as my sister.

Slowly it dawned on me that I was placing too much hope in my membership in the Carmelite Order, and not enough in God alone. If God called me to let go of my OCDS vocation, he would grant grace for the spiritual road ahead through my obedience and acceptance. It was time to let go—again.

I sent a second e-mail to the provincial delegate, telling him that since he could make no exceptions for me about meeting requirements, the order would have to release me from my promise. I received no reply.

I had no plans at that time to blog on Carmelite spirituality or write books about Carmelite saints. I could not know that in a short while I would be more immersed in Carmelite writings than ever before. And I had no idea that I could avoid Purgatory without performing all the extra, meritorious acts I had once read about.

I had to leave the Carmelite Order before I could understand what being a Carmelite was really about.

That is the place I find myself in today, three years later. I am starting my spiritual life over, founding it on trust in God alone.

Dying to one's trust

We have covered a lot of territory in our exploration of trusting God. We have learned we can trust him with our past. He will help us move beyond the shortcomings of our parents or other caregivers. Instead of blaming those who have hurt us, we can forgive. He will bring good out of our tragedies, if we allow him to. We can even become the good in tragic situations when we surrender ourselves to him.

When God makes us wait, as he repeatedly made Therese wait, we can do so peacefully. Calmly working and praying to achieve our goal, we can leave the results and the timing to him.

Sins and weaknesses should never shake our confidence. Instead, they can teach us to rely solely on his goodness. When anger, fear, or sorrow threaten our peace, we can pray, "Jesus, I trust in you." Embracing our spiritual darkness, we can let go of confidence in our insights, feelings, or gifts.

We know now that Jesus can be trusted with the future. Hoping against hope, we will see him bring life out of death and hardened sinners to conversion. We can have hope of avoiding Purgatory, not because of our merits, but because of his delight in accomplishing the desires he places in our hearts.

We have come a certain distance in our understanding of trust. We have begun to practice it. Now a new threat arises. We might think we understand everything. *Ah!* we tell ourselves, *The spiritual life is all about trust. No problem. I can do that.* Confident in our confidence, like the Apostle Peter in the Gospel, we ask Jesus to help us walk on water. But then we take our eyes off of Jesus and look at the wind and waves. We begin to sink. "Help, Lord, I'm drowning!" we cry. And all the time he is right there beside us.

Until the end of her life, Therese had confidence in Jesus, but not in her own confidence. She would not trust in her faithfulness to the little way.

> Someone told me that I shall fear death. This could very well be true. There isn't anyone here more mistrustful of her feelings than I am. I never rely on my own ideas; I know how weak I am. (LC 46)

Thoughts that she might falter did not disturb her at all. She trusted God to fill up what was lacking in her trust. She might well be unfaithful before the end. But she had no fear that God would be unfaithful to her.

> I haven't any misgivings whatsoever about the final struggles or sufferings of this sickness, no matter how great they may be. God has always come to my aid; He has helped me and led me by the hand from my childhood. I count upon Him, I'm sure He will continue to help me until the end. I may really become exhausted and worn out, but I shall never have too much to suffer; I'm sure of this. (LC 50)

Therese echoed these words of St. Paul, "I am sure that he who began a good work in you will bring it to completion at the day of Jesus Christ" (Phil 1:6).

When Mother Agnes expressed her fear that Therese would suffer unbearably before she died, Therese replied, "Why fear in advance? Wait at least for it to happen before having any distress" (LC 100).

Therese's last hours

The Thief, as the Martin sisters referred to our Lord, took his time in coming for Therese, but at last he arrived. On Wednesday morning, September 29, Therese's throat began to rattle, a common sign that death was at hand. Mother Marie de Gonzague gathered all the nuns around Therese's bed to recite the prayers for the dying. Then she dismissed them.

Later, Dr. de Corniere came for his final visit. When he had gone, Therese asked the prioress "Is it today, Mother?" (LC 204).

"Yes, my child," Mother Marie de Gonzague answered.

One of the nuns present said that God was very glad that day, for Therese would be coming to him. "I am glad too," Therese answered. "If I were to die right now, what happiness!" (ibid.)

Sr. Marie of the Trinity, the "novice of the shell," came to visit, but Therese sent her away. She regretted it almost immediately, fearing she should have let the other nun stay. Mother Agnes reassured her.

The convent's chaplain, Abbé Youf, was also seriously ill. He would die not long after Therese. So Abbé Faucon, the extraordinary confessor, came in his stead to hear Therese's final confession.

That night, contrary to custom and to Therese's wishes, Mother Marie de Gonzague ordered Sr. Marie of the Sacred Heart and Sr. Genevieve to stay with Therese all night in the infirmary, taking turns sleeping. Meanwhile, Mother Agnes retired to Genevieve's cell next door and tried to sleep. She had a splitting headache from the strain of sitting with Therese.

Marie gave Therese a glass of water in the night, and fell asleep before Therese could hand it back to her. She woke to find her sister still holding the glass with a trembling hand, unwilling to disturb her sleep.

The next day was filled with "veritable torments," according to Mother Agnes (LC 204). Therese confirmed that she was experiencing pure suffering, with no consolations. She said to Mother Marie de Gonzague, "Oh mother, I assure you, the chalice is filled to the brim!" (LC 205). And yet she later said, "All that I wrote about my desires for suffering. Oh! It's true just the same." She continued on after catching what breath she still could, "And I am not sorry for delivering myself up to Love" (ibid.).

It was nearing five in the evening, when Mother Agnes, the only one with her at the time, noticed a change in her face and knew that the final agony had come. She notified the community, who gathered around the bed once more. Therese was holding a crucifix and staring at it. Still, she struggled for two hours, her face and limbs turning blue and purple as less and less oxygen entered her body. Sweat soaked her clothes and the sheets beneath her.

Finally, she fell back on the pillow, and Mother Marie de Gonzague ordered the doors to be opened. The nuns knelt around her bed. Then Therese's face became white again. She gazed at a spot on the wall as if she were seeing heavenly sights. This lasted half a minute. Then she smiled and breathed her last.

Therese had stated that she wanted to spend her heaven doing good for souls still on the earth (SL 197). Once Marie of the Sacred Heart had exclaimed about how sad they would be when Therese died. She replied, "Oh, no, you will see; it will be like a shower of roses" (LC 62). She had often strewn petals of roses before a crucifix as a symbol of her love offerings to Jesus. In heaven she would do the opposite. Standing by the side of Jesus, she would toss rose petals of love toward her sisters still on earth.

Her mission did not end with her death. It began in earnest. She is not content to rest until the last sinner has placed his confidence in God. She showers down roses upon all of us who seek to trust and love him. Always, everything for souls. Never anything for herself except Jesus. He was and is her all-in-all.

Until eternity

When my parents choose a tombstone for my sister Terri, they decided on the epitaph, "Our flower blooms in heaven." I like to think that in heaven Terri is friends with her patron saint Therese. Together they worship God with the simplicity of children. Together they pray for me. Together they urge me on to trust God to make my path smooth.

I do not know what the future will bring for good or evil. Unexpected sorrows and joys may both lie ahead. Whatever turns my road takes, however many times I stall or crash, I trust God to bring me safely at last, in his way and time, to heaven.

Questions for Reflection

1. Have I been settling for a place in Purgatory, rather than hoping to go straight to heaven?

2. Do I believe that Therese was right about Purgatory, or does it seem too presumptuous?

3. Am I afraid of seeing God face to face on Judgment Day? Can I begin to think of him as a loving Father, rather than a Judge?

Practical Suggestions

* Choose one of Therese's quotes about Purgatory or God's mercy to copy and post somewhere you will see it daily. Read it over to yourself often.

* Go back through this book and review the Questions for Reflection at the end of each chapter. How has your attitude changed since you first started reading it?

* Choose one Practical Suggestion from anywhere in this book that you skipped on your first reading and practice it today.

A Brief Timeline of the Life of St. Therese

1873 Thursday, January 2 – Therese is born in Alençon, France.
Tuesday, March 11 – Rose Taillé takes Therese to her farm for nursing.

1874 Thursday, April 2 – Therese returns home to Alençon on Holy Thursday.

1877 Saturday, February 24 – Therese's aunt Sr. Marie-Dosithée dies.
Tuesday, August 28 – Zelie Martin dies of breast cancer.
Thursday, November 15 – The Martin family moves to Les Buissonnets in Lisieux.

1882 Monday, October 2 – Pauline Martin enters the Carmelite cloister in Lisieux. She later takes the name Agnes of Jesus.

1883 Sunday, May 13 – On this Pentecost Sunday, a smile form the statue of Our Lady of Victory marks Therese's cure from a serious illness.

1884 Thursday, May 8 – Therese's first Communion and Sr. Agnes' profession of vows.

1886 February or March – Therese leaves the Abbey school and continues her studies under tutor Madame Papinau.
Friday, October 15 – Marie Martin enters the Carmelite cloister, later taking the name Marie of the Sacred Heart.
Saturday, December 25 – Therese experiences her Christmas conversion.

1887 Sunday, May 1 – Louis Martin suffers his first stroke.
Sunday, May 29 – On Pentecost, Louis Martin gives his permission for Therese to enter Carmel.
Summer – Celine and Therese pray for Pranzini's conversion.
Monday, October 31 – Louis and Therese visit Msgr. Hugonin, bishop of Bayeux, to ask permission for early entrance into Carmel.
Friday, November 4 to Friday, December 2 – Louis, Celine, and

Therese join the pilgrimage to Rome.
Sunday, November 20 – Therese asks Pope Leo XIII for permission to enter Carmel early.

1888 Monday, April 9 – On the feast of the Annunciation, Therese enters Carmel. She later takes the name Therese of the Child Jesus and the Holy Face.
Tuesday, May 22 – Marie makes her vows.
Sunday, May 28 –Therese confesses to Fr. Pichon.
Saturday, June 23 – Louis Martin runs away to Le Havre.

1889 Thursday, January 10 – Therese becomes a novice.
Tuesday, February 12 – Louis Martin enters the Bon Sauveur Mental Hospital in Caen.

1890 Monday, September 8 – Therese makes her vows.

1892 January – Influenza epidemic ravages the Carmel of Lisieux.
Tuesday, May 10 – Louis Martin leaves the hospital and lives with the Guerin family.
Thursday, May 12 – Louis sees his Carmelite daughters for the last time.

1893 Monday, February 20 – Sister Agnes is elected prioress.
September – Therese requests and receives permission to remain in the novitiate for life.

1894 Sunday, July 29 – Louis Martin dies while at the seaside with the Guerins and his daughter Celine.
Tuesday, September 14 – Celine Martin enters the cloister and later takes the name Genevieve of the Holy Face.

1895 Therese writes Manuscript A of *Story of a Soul* at the direction of Mother Agnes.
Sunday, June 9 – On Trinity Sunday, Therese is inspired to make the Oblation to Merciful Love. She and Sr. Genevieve do so two days later.
Thursday, August 15 – Marie Guerin enters the cloister, later taking the name Marie of the Eucharist.
Thursday, October 17 – Fr. Belliere becomes Therese's first "spiritual brother."

1896 Saturday, March 21 – Mother Marie de Gonzague is re-elected prioress. She appoints Therese as assistant to the novice mistress (herself).

Friday, April 3 – Early on Good Friday, Therese coughs up blood for the first time.

Sunday, April 5 – On Easter, Therese's final spiritual darkness descends.

Saturday, May 30– Fr. Roulland becomes Therese's second "spiritual brother."

Tuesday, September 8 – Therese writes Manuscript B of *Story of a Soul* at the request of Sr. Marie of the Sacred Heart.

1897 Tuesday, April 6 – Mother Agnes begins recording Therese's words in what will become the first part of *Last Conversations.*

June to July – Therese writes Manuscript C of *Story of a Soul* as directed by Mother Marie de Gonzague.

Thursday, July 8 – Therese enters the infirmary.

Friday, July 30 – Therese receives the Anointing of the Sick.

Thursday, September 30 – Therese dies in the evening.

1925 Sunday, May 17 – Pope Pius XI canonizes Therese.

1997 Sunday, October 19 – Pope John Paul II declares St. Therese a Doctor of the Church.

Who's Who in the Life of St. Therese

Belliere, Fr. –Therese's first "spiritual brother," a missionary priest with whom she corresponded. Also called Canon Belliere.

de Corniere, Dr. Alexandre-Damase – The doctor who attended Therese in her final illness.

Delatroette, Fr. – Superior of the Lisieux Carmel at the time of Therese's entrance. He died in 1895. Also called Canon Delatroette.

Domin, Abbé – Chaplain and confessor at the Benedictine boarding school the Martin girls attended.

Ducellier, Fr. Alcide – Pastor of St. Peter's Cathedral in Lisieux. He heard Therese's first confession and gave the first sermon she understood.

Faucon, Abbé – Extraordinary confessor for the Carmelite nuns. He heard Therese's final confession.

Guerin, Celine – Wife of Isidore Guerin.
Isidore – Therese's uncle and guardian.
Jeanne – Elder daughter of Isidore and Celine Guerin. She married Francis La Neele
Marie – The younger daughter of Isidore and Celine Guerin, she became Sr. Marie of the Eucharist.
Marie-Azelie. *See* Martin, Zelie.
Marie-Louise – Therese's aunt. She became a Dominican nun and took the name Marie-Dosithée.

Hugonin, Msgr. – Bishop of Bayeux, France, the diocese containing Lisieux during the life of Therese.

La Neele, Dr. Francis – The husband of Therese's cousin Jeanne, he examined Therese on her deathbed when Dr. de Corniere was out of town.
Jeanne. *See* Guerin, Jeanne.

Leo XIII – The pope who told Therese that she would enter Carmel early, "if God wills it."

Leriche, Adolphe – Nephew of Louis Martin, he bought Louis' watch and jewelry shop.
Marie – Wife of Adolphe. She cared for little Celine and Therese while their mother Zelie was dying.

Martin, Celine – The fourth surviving child of the Martin family, Therese's closest companion. She was known in Carmel as Sr. Genevieve of the Holy Face.
Helene – Therese's sister who died of a sudden illness at age five.
Leonie – The third Martin daughter. She was in and out of convents before finally becoming a Visitation sister, known as Sr. Françoise-Therese.
Louis – The father of Therese. He was beatified by Pope Benedict XVI.
Marie – The eldest daughter of Louis and Zelie. She raised Therese after Pauline entered the convent. In Carmel she took the name Sr. Marie of the Sacred Heart.
Marie-Azelie. *See* Martin, Zelie.
Marie-Françoise-Therese – *See* Martin, Therese.
Marie-Joseph-Jean-Baptist – A son of Louis and Zelie who died as an infant.
Marie-Joseph-Louis – A son of Louis and Zelie who died as an infant.
Marie-Melanie-Therese – An infant daughter of Louis and Zelie who died of malnutrition.
Pauline – The second of Therese's sisters. She later became Mother Agnes of Jesus.
Therese – Born Marie-Françoise-Therese. She became Therese of the Child Jesus and the Holy Face in Carmel, and became a saint known for her little way of spiritual childhood.
Zelie – The mother of Therese. She was beatified by Pope Benedict XVI.

Maudelonde, Ernest – A relative of the Guerins who helped Isidore Guerin search for Louis Martin when he ran away to Le Havre.

Maupas, Canon – He succeeded Fr. Delatroette as superior of the Lisieux Carmel.

Mother Agnes of Jesus – *See* Martin, Pauline.
Genevieve of St. Teresa – Foundress of the Lisieux Carmel.

Marie de Gonzague – Prioress for most of Therese's life in Carmel.

Notta, Dr. Alphonse-Henri – He attended Zelie Martin in her final illness and Therese in her illness at age ten.

Pichon, Fr. – Spiritual director to Marie Martin until his departure for Canada in 1888, he heard Therese's general confession and proclaimed God's mercy.

Pranzini, Henri – A convicted murderer who kissed a crucifix on the scaffold after Therese and Celine prayed and sacrificed for his conversion.

Sister Febronie – Subprioress from the time of Therese's entrance until Febronie died in the flu epidemic of 1892.
Françoise-Therese. *See* Martin, Leonie.
Genevieve of the Holy Face. *See* Martin, Celine.
Marguerite-Marie – A hard-working, but mentally ill nun, she ultimately had to leave the convent.
Marie-Dosithée – *See* Guerin, Marie-Louise.
Marie-Madeleine – A novice who avoided opening up to Therese for direction. She had been traumatized earlier in life.
Marie of St. Joseph – The laundress who splashed Therese and so taught her how to love difficult people. She later had to leave the convent due to mental illness.
Marie of the Angels – Novice mistress when Therese entered Carmel. She also spent time as subprioress.
Marie of the Eucharist – *See* Guerin, Marie.
Marie of the Sacred Heart – *See* Martin, Marie.
Marie of the Trinity – A novice under Therese's direction. She could not control her tears until Therese told her to cry into a shell.
Marie-Philomene – A nun who left the convent while a postulant in order to nurse her sick mother and had to wait nine years for permission to re-enter.
St. Pierre – The elderly sister Therese helped from the choir to the refectory every day for seven years.
St. Stanislaus – The infirmarian during Therese's years in Carmel.
St. Vincent de Paul – A nun who called Therese "the grand lady" and criticized her embroidery. She famously wondered what

the convent could possibly write in Therese's circular after her death.

Therese of the Child Jesus and the Holy Face – *See* Martin, Therese.

Therese of St. Augustine – A nun with a difficult temperament who was convinced she was Therese's best friend.

Reverony, Msgr. – Vicar general of the Diocese of Bayeux, France, who led the pilgrimage to Rome in 1887.

Roulland, Fr. – Therese's second "spiritual brother," a missionary priest she began corresponding with shortly before her death.

Taillé, Rose – Therese's wet nurse. Also known as Rosalie Taillé.

Youf, Abbé – Regular confessor for the Carmel of Lisieux during Therese's time there.

Note to the Reader

If you have enjoyed reading *Trusting God with St. Therese*, please consider writing a review on the book's page at Amazon.com. God reward you!

Acknowledgements

God's blessings on all who have helped me with their work, prayers, and advice in writing and publishing this book. I'd like to thank several people in particular: my husband, Dan Rossini, for his patience and editing expertise; the Carmelite nuns of Lisieux, for all the material from their archives that they have made available through their website, and for generously answering my questions about texts; Gary Zimak, Donna-Marie Cooper O'Boyle, Sarah Reinhard, and Devin Rose, for their endorsements; the members of my non-fiction critique group, especially Nancy Ward; my beta readers, Mary Nicewarmer, Michael Incorvia, Mallory Hoffman, and Melanie Jean Juneau; the members of my Google+ Community, Indie Catholic Authors; and the Catholic Writers Guild. This book is a tribute to your support, prayers, and hard work on my behalf.

Connect with the Author

Connie Rossini blogs at contemplativehomeschool.com. For more on the spirituality of St. Therese, and updates on future writing projects, subscribe to her blog posts.

You can follow Connie on Twitter as @ConnieRossini. Join the conversation about this book at twubs.com/TrustingGodBook or by using #TrustingGodBook.

To view dozens of pictures related to St. Therese, trusting God, and Connie's memoirs, visit her Pinterest Boards at pinterest.com/connierossini/.

You can also find Connie at:

facebook.com/connie.rossini.9
google.com/+ConnieRossini
linkedin.com/in/connierossini

Made in the USA
San Bernardino, CA
30 March 2015